Cambridge Elements

Elements in Semantics
edited by
Jonathan Ginzburg
Université Paris-Cité
Daniel Lassiter
University of Edinburgh

REDUCTION AND UNIFICATION IN NATURAL LANGUAGE ONTOLOGY

Kristina Liefke
Ruhr University Bochum

CAMBRIDGE
UNIVERSITY PRESS

Shaftesbury Road, Cambridge CB2 8EA, United Kingdom

One Liberty Plaza, 20th Floor, New York, NY 10006, USA

477 Williamstown Road, Port Melbourne, VIC 3207, Australia

314–321, 3rd Floor, Plot 3, Splendor Forum, Jasola District Centre, New Delhi – 110025, India

103 Penang Road, #05–06/07, Visioncrest Commercial, Singapore 238467

Cambridge University Press is part of Cambridge University Press & Assessment, a department of the University of Cambridge.

We share the University's mission to contribute to society through the pursuit of education, learning and research at the highest international levels of excellence.

www.cambridge.org
Information on this title: www.cambridge.org/9781009559645

DOI: 10.1017/9781009559683

When citing this work, please include a reference to the DOI 10.1017/9781009559683

First published 2024

A catalogue record for this publication is available from the British Library.

ISBN 978-1-009-55964-5 Hardback
ISBN 978-1-009-55965-2 Paperback
ISSN 2754-0367 (online)
ISSN 2754-0359 (print)

Reduction and Unification in Natural Language Ontology

Elements in Semantics

DOI: 10.1017/9781009559683
First published online: December 2024

Kristina Liefke
Ruhr University Bochum

Author for correspondence: Kristina Liefke,
Kristina.Liefke@ruhr-uni-bochum.de

Abstract: Semantic theories for natural language assume many different kinds of objects, including (among many others) individuals, properties, events, degrees, and kinds. Formal type-theoretic semantics tames this 'zoo' of objects by assuming only a small number of ontologically primitive categories and by obtaining the objects of all other categories through constructions out of these primitives. This Element surveys arguments for this reduction of semantic categories. It compares the ontological commitments of different such reductions and establishes relations between competing foundational semantic ontologies. In doing so, it yields insights into the requirements on minimal semantic ontologies for natural language and the challenges for semantic ontology engineering.

Keywords: ontology, compositional semantics, categories, type systems, semantic ontology engineering

ISBNs: 9781009559645 (HB) 9781009559652 (PB) 9781009559683 (OC)
ISSNs: 2754-0367 (online), 2754-0359 (print)

Contents

> [An] overpopulated universe . . . offends the aesthetic sense of us who have a taste for desert landscapes, but this is not the worst of it.
>
> (Quine, 1948, 23)

1 Introduction

Natural languages presuppose a rich semantic ontology. For example, to interpret the English sentence *Matti is neatly tying a knot*, most contemporary semantic theories assume individuals (i.e. Matti, a particular knot), properties of individuals (i.e. being a knot), events (i.e. tying a knot), manners (i.e. neatly), and times (or time intervals; e.g. the interval in which Matti is tying the knot). To interpret other sentences or linguistic expressions (e.g. *Matti is 1.43 m tall*), these theories even introduce further objects and ontological categories, like degrees (i.e. 1.43 m).

Natural language ontology – or, more aptly, the ontology of natural language *semantics* – identifies the classes of objects that are assumed by our best semantic theories (see e.g. Ginzburg, 2008; Liefke, 2024b; Moltmann, 2022; Rett, 2022). Specifically, it seeks to show which ontological categories are part of "the semanticist's toolbox" (Rett, 2022, p. 281) (s.t. they are included in the most common semantic models) and "what . . . relations among them [are needed] to exhibit the structure of meanings that natural languages seem to have" (Bach, 1986b, 573). To meet this goal, natural language ontology

(i) provides a domain of nonlinguistic objects (which serve as the meanings, or 'semantic values,' of natural language expressions);
(ii) sorts these objects according to their ontological and semantic (e.g. truth-contributional, selection, and entailment) properties; and
(iii) explains how objects with similar such properties interact with other objects to yield new objects (with yet different properties).

Steps (i) and (ii) identify the *descriptive ontology* of natural language(s) that reflects a practitioner's view of natural language ontology. The latter is a rich ontology that includes the semantic values of all (simple and complex) linguistic expressions (Step (i)). It is built from an unstructured domain of ontological 'wildlife' in which the semantic values of linguistic expressions roam free without any classification or constraints. This domain contains objects like Matti and his particular knot alongside intuitively different types of entities, like properties (e.g. being a knot) and events (e.g. tying a knot).

Ontological categories like 'individual,' 'property,' and 'event' are obtained in a second step (i.e. Step (ii)) which co-classifies similar – or similarly behaved – objects (e.g. Matti, the knot). It is these categories that are used to explain syntactic/semantic selection (e.g. why (1a) is not an acceptable expression of English) and to account for restrictions on the binding of certain pronouns (e.g. why *Tying a constrictor knot* cannot bind the pronoun *he* in (1b)).

(1) a. *Matti carefully

b. [Tying a constrictor knot]$_i$ made Matti's brain hurt. {$^{\#}$He$_i$,$^{\checkmark}$It$_i$} made Sam break into sweat.

This Element focuses on the *foundational ontology* of natural language semantics that is obtained through a systematic investigation of the descriptive ontology that results from (i) and (ii). This investigation involves identifying relations between objects from different semantic categories (see Step (iii)) and reducing the 'zoo' of categories from the descriptive ontology to a small(er) set of basic categories.

From a semantic point of view, foundational interest in natural language ontology is motivated by the need to provide a sensible account of meaning composition: Unless our semantic theories assume that individuals are, in some interesting way, related to properties (viz. through property exemplification), they cannot explain why the semantic value of the proper name *Matti*, that is ⟦Matti⟧, composes with the value of the predicate *tie a knot*, that is ⟦tie a knot⟧, to form a larger meaningful unit (e.g. a proposition; see e.g. Lewis, 1972; Partee, 1983). Other useful relations of this sort include individuals partaking in events, propositions being true at (or 'holding in') possible worlds/times, and events showing (or 'illustrating') manners. An example of an ontology that explicitly marks such inter-category relations (due to Champollion, 2017) is included in Figure 1.

Inter-category relations like the ones in Figure 1 even serve a larger methodological purpose: they can help identify the basic ontological building blocks of our semantic theories. These building blocks are semantic categories from which we can obtain all other descriptive categories through the familiar operations (e.g. set/class formation, function space formation, products). Identifying these building blocks has a number of important merits: Firstly, it hardcodes inter-category relations (viz. by defining some, 'derived' [= non-basic], categories in terms of other, more basic, categories) and, thus, enables a straightforward account of the meaningful- or meaninglessness of complex expressions (see my elaborations in Sections 3.1–3.2). Secondly, it increases our semantics' ontological parsimony (s.t. the resulting ontology contains as few basic categories as are required for semantic modeling; see Section 3.3).

An example of such increase in parsimony is given in (3b). This increase is achieved by analyzing properties as (time-parametrized) sets of individuals

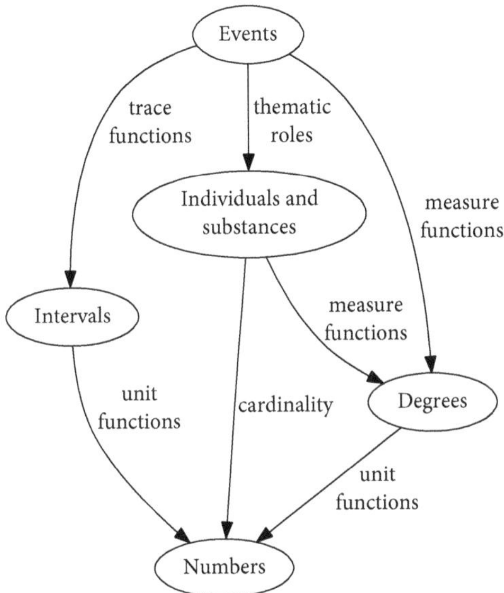

Figure 1 Examples of inter-category relations from (Champollion 2017, 25).

(following Armstrong, 1980; see Montague, 1970) and by analyzing manners as similarity classes of events (following Umbach & Gust, 2014). By adopting these analyses, semantic theories reduce the ontological commitment of sentence (2) (originally, (3a)) by two categories (viz. properties and manners; see (3b)).

(2) Matti is neatly tying a knot.

(3) a. {individuals, events, **properties**, **manners**, times, . . .}
$\subset$ b. {individuals, events, times, . . .}

It is sometimes argued that observations about the semantic ontology of natural language can yield insights into the fundamental building blocks of reality (Bach, 1986b; Davidson, 1977). While I am skeptical about the general reliability of this language-based approach to metaphysics, I believe that some (!) basic semantic categories may well turn out to be promising candidates for 'what there [really] is' (to use the term from Quine, 1948). These will likely be categories (e.g. individuals) whose assumption is also supported by other approaches to metaphysical knowledge (like the experience-, the common sense-, or the science-based approach; see Meixner, 2011; Ney, 2014).

Importantly, the real-world existence of the objects in question does not yet provide a strong argument for a category's admission into our minimal semantic models. This holds, for example, of properties, which are assumed by many common-belief- and (natural) scientific models, but are excluded as basic objects in the majority of models from formal semantics.[1] In this sense, natural language ontology is more selective than mainstream philosophical metaphysics. In this Element, I hope to show that the restriction to the smallest set of categories that can still generate the full descriptive ontology has a number of remarkable merits.

To obtain such ‘minimal’ semantic ontologies, this Element uses the standard tool, namely type theory (Church, 1940; see also Bach, 1986b; Montague, 1970). The latter is a powerful formal framework that allows us to ‘tame’ the descriptive ontological zoo into a pocket-size collection of a few basic categories. The Element is structured as follows: To provide the necessary background for applying type theory to the descriptive ontology of natural language, Section 2 surveys different strategies for identifying a language’s semantic commitments and characterizes the descriptive (!) ontologies that result from applying these strategies to some familiar natural language fragments (esp. to Montague’s PTQ-fragment and to its event-semantic extensions).

Section 3 reviews the linguistic merits of typing the objects in a language’s semantic ontology. Section 4 introduces the core tools and assumptions of simple type theory (Church, 1940; Gallin, 1975) and uses this theory to illustrate the merits of typing from Section 3. Section 5 compares the different type systems that have been used to provide a semantics for Montague’s (1973) PTQ-fragment, focusing on the systems IL (Montague, 1970, 1973), TY_2 (Gallin, 1975), and a version of TY_1 (Kaplan, 1976; Montague, 1974).[2] These systems take some few ontological categories (in the case of Montague, 1974: individuals and propositions) as basic, and construct the members of all other categories (e.g. first- and higher-order properties) from objects of these basic types through special type-forming rules. Section 6 discusses the effects of applying simple type theories to the descriptive ontologies of larger natural language fragments.

Section 7 extends empirical arguments for the reduction of semantic categories by methodological considerations. These considerations start from the observation that genuinely more parsimonious ontologies require a unification of semantic categories. The section presents two recent efforts in this direction, that is inquisitive semantics (Ciardelli, Groenendijk, & Roelofsen, 2018;

[1] Exceptions are Keenan’s (2015, 2018) ‘individual-free’ semantics as well as Property Theory (e.g. Chierchia, 1984; Chierchia & Turner, 1988), California-style situation semantics (Barwise & Perry, 1983), and Type Theory with Records (TTR) (Cooper, 2012; Cooper & Ginzburg, 2015).

[2] This Element exclusively focuses on simple type systems. For an introduction to semantics with modern/rich type systems (which use a larger number of type constructors, and in which types are part of the object language), the reader is referred to the Element in Semantics by Chatzikyriakidis et al. (2025) (see also Chatzikyriakidis & Luo, 2020; Sutton, 2024).

Theiler, Roelofsen, & Aloni, 2018) and single-type semantics (Liefke, 2014; Liefke & Werning, 2018; Partee, 2009). From these efforts, it draws a number of lessons about the trade-off between simplicity and parsimony, the relation between the ontological object- and metatheory, and about the engineering of semantic ontologies more generally. The Element closes by reviewing its findings and by emphasizing how inter-ontology relations can yield insights into the foundational semantic ontology of natural language.

Before I present the descriptive background of this Element (in Section 2), it is important to add a note on terminology, and a caveat about the language- and theory-specificity of semantic ontology.

1.1 Terminology and a Caveat

My previous discussion has already suggested that the term 'ontology' can be used to refer both to a scientific discipline and to its topic of study, that is the semantic ontology of natural language. (The latter, but not the former, consists of different ontological categories like 'individual' and 'property.') Since the noun *ontology* has a plural form (i.e. *ontologies*), it in principle allows for the possibility that the subject matter of natural language ontology differs from language to language, or from semantic theory to semantic theory. (Both are indeed the case, as I show in the remainder of this subsection.) To avoid having the term 'natural language ontology' do double duty, this Element follows Moltmann (2022) in using 'natural language ontology' for the discipline and 'semantic ontology of natural language' (shortened 'semantic ontology' or, simply, 'ontology') for the subject matter of this discipline.

That the subject matter of natural language ontology differs from language to language is illustrated by contemporary semantics for the pair of sentences in (4). This pair comprises a German sentence with an explicit comparative (*ist größer als* ['is taller than']; in (4a)) and its closest possible translation in Motu, an Austronesian language of Papua New Guinea (in (4b); based on Beck et al., 2009).

(4) a. Matti ist größer als Cleo. (German)
'Matti is taller than Cleo.'

b. Matti na lata, to Cleo na kwadōgi. (Motu)
Matti TOP tall, but Cleo TOP short.
'Matti is tall, but Cleo is short.'

Expectedly, the occurrence of proper names (i.e. *Matti*, *Cleo*) in the two sentences incurs a common commitment – in German and in Motu – to individuals. Many contemporary semantics argue that the intuitive truth-conditions of constructions with the comparative morpheme *-er* further require a commitment to degrees, d (see the interpretation of (4a) in (5), where '$\mu_{\text{height}}(\mathbf{matti})$' is the degree to which Matti is tall; see e.g. Lassiter, 2012; Rett, 2022).

(5) $(\exists d)[(\mu_{\text{height}}(\mathbf{matti}) \geq d) \wedge \neg(\mu_{\text{height}}(\mathbf{cleo}) \geq d)]$

In contrast to German, Motu lacks a dedicated degree morphology and does not allow difference comparatives. To compensate for the nonavailability of comparative morphology, Motu speakers use a conjunctive strategy that juxtaposes two full clauses with antonymous predicates. Beck et al. (2009) have shown that a suitable semantics for the resulting constructions (e.g. (4b)) requires neither a measure function nor a degree variable (see also Bochnak, 2015). Instead, they interpret gradable predicates like *tall* as context-sensitive vague predicates (viz. 'counts as tall in c'; see (6)).

(6) $\mathbf{tall}(c, \mathbf{matti}) \wedge \mathbf{short}(c, \mathbf{cleo})$

Beck's semantics suggests that, in contrast to the semantic ontology of (4a), the ontology of (4a)'s Motu counterpart, (4b), does not contain degrees. The local [= German] ontology of (4a) (in (7b)) hence properly includes the local [= Motu] ontology of (4b) (in (7a)):

(7) a. Motu-[(4b), Beck et al., 2009]: {individuals, properties}
$\subset$ b. German-[(4a), Lassiter, 2012]: {individuals, properties, **degrees**}

To avoid leaving ontologies underspecified with respect to the interpreted language or fragment, this Element will be explicit about the language for which it provides a semantic ontology. Whenever no language is specified, ontological claims will be relative to a reasonably representative fragment of contemporary American English (that extends Montague's PTQ-fragment). Since there is a large overlap between the semantic ontology of this extended fragment of English and representative fragments of other languages (incl. Motu), I expect that the findings from this Element will also be relevant for the local ontologies of other languages, and for the global semantic ontology (which is shared by all natural languages).

I have mentioned at the beginning of this subsection that language-specific (i.e. 'local') semantic ontologies still vary with the particular semantic theory that is adopted for the respective language. This is so since different semantic theories may – at least in part – assume objects from different semantic categories. A key example of this observation can be found in the difference between contemporary degree-based semantics for comparatives (e.g. Cresswell, 1976; Lassiter, 2012; von Stechow, 1984) and earlier degree-free approaches (e.g. Klein, 1980; McConnell-Ginet, 1973; Neeleman, van de Koot, & Doetjes, 2004): Since degree-free approaches analyze degrees as equivalence classes of individuals (and, hence, drop degrees from their stock of basic entities), they ascribe English and German a Motu-style semantic ontology:

(8) a. Motu-[(4b), Beck et al., 2009]: {individuals, properties}
$\stackrel{!}{=}$ b. German-[(4a), Klein, 1980]: {individuals, properties}

The effect of semantic theory on local ontology is further illustrated by the difference between Beck's (2009) and a Keenan (2015)-style interpretation of (7a)/(8a). Since Keenan's semantics interprets proper names as sets of primitive [= non-decomposable] properties (see also Keenan, 2018; Keenan & Faltz, 1985), its application to (7a) would waive Motu's commitment to individuals (see (9a)).

(9) a. German-[(4a), Keenan, 2015]: {properties, **degrees**}
$\supset$ b. Motu-[(4b), Keenan, 2015]: {properties}
$\subset$ c. Motu-[(4b), Beck et al., 2009]: {**individuals**, properties}

The difference between (7b), (7a)/(8)/(9c), (9a), and (9b) illustrates that specifying a local semantic ontology requires identifying both (i) the interpreted language (or fragment) and (ii) the particular semantic theory that is adopted for its interpretation.

Ritchie (2016) has proposed to remedy the dependence on a semantic theory by adopting a Principle of Carrying Commitments (PCC). This principle assumes that, in determining a language's ontological commitments, semantics with equal empirical adequacy should be given an equal voice (see Ritchie, 2016, 20). In virtue of this assumption, it holds that a (language or) linguistic phenomenon only determinately carries a commitment to a certain ontological category if *all* competing semantic theories for this phenomenon carry this commitment. For example, since the ontologies in (7a)/(9c) and (9b) only agree with respect to properties, PCC's application to the Motu sentence (4b) only determines an ontological commitment to properties. Since degree-free semantics for explicit comparatives fail to satisfy Ritchie's adequacy requirement,[3] PCC determines an additional commitment to degrees when applied to the German sentence (4a) (see the larger intersection of (7b) and (9a)).

I will return to PCC in the later parts of this Element, where I apply this criterion to different intensional ontologies (in Section 5.3) and where I modify PCC to a criterion that respects the difference between ontologies of the semantic object- and the metatheory (in Section 8). In the meantime, I will exploit an

[3] For a discussion of the shortcomings of these semantic theories, the reader is referred to Gehrke and Castroviejo (2015) as well as Schäfer (2006).

ontology's variance with (ii) in Sections 6 and 7. Since this exploitation will yield insights into the minimal requirements on a given language's semantic ontology, it will inform the modification from Section 8.

2 Descriptive Natural Language Ontology

My previous discussion has treated the descriptive ontologies of contemporary semantics for (some fragment of) English as essentially given. The present section takes a step back, taking a closer look at how semantic theories might arrive at the local ontologies that will be presupposed in Sections 4 to 7. To do this, it first surveys different strategies that have been used to identify a language's semantic commitments (in Section 2.1). It then sketches the descriptive ontologies that result from applying these strategies to Montague's PTQ-fragment (in Section 2.2) and to some of its contemporary extensions (in Section 2.3).

NOTE: This section is a quick version of Sections 2 to 4 of the prequel Element, *Natural Language Ontology and Semantic Theory* (Liefke, 2024b). For a slower, more detailed, presentation of the material that also includes a survey of the relevant background (e.g. the syntax-semantics homomorphism, the method of indirect interpretation), the reader is referred to the prequel Element.

2.1 Identifying a Language's Semantic Commitments

In what follows, I review three strategies for identifying a language's descriptive ontological commitments. These strategies are based on the semantic selection properties of natural language predicates (see Section 2.1.1), on the study of dedicated proforms and quantifiers (see Section 2.1.2), and on the identification of implicit semantic arguments (see Section 2.1.3).

2.1.1 The Lexical Strategy: Selection Properties

A first strategy for identifying a language's semantic commitments investigates differences in the semantic selection properties of predicates. Following Vendler (1967a, 1967b), this strategy assumes that selectional differences track ontological differences in the kinds of arguments that these predicates combine with. According to this strategy, a predicate's ability to accept only one, but not the other of two expressions as a semantic argument suggests that these expressions belong to different ontological categories.

A simple instance of this strategy is given in (10). This instance investigates the possibility of combining the predicate *occur* with different syntactic arguments – in particular: with the nominal gerund *John's singing* (see (10b)), with the referential DP *John* (or *the boy*; see (10a)), and with the declarative sentence (or clause) *(that) John was singing* (see (10c)). Since the result of this combination is deviant for the two last-mentioned arguments (as marked by superscript question marks in (10a/c)), the strategy concludes that the semantic values of *John/the boy* and of *(that) John was singing* must belong to a different ontological category than the semantic value of *John's singing*. Since *occur* expresses a temporal property (which requires its semantic arguments to be temporal or temporally located objects), Vendler (1967b) identifies semantic arguments like *John's singing* in (10b) with an event (see also Grimm & McNally, 2022).

(10) a. ??John/the boy
b. John's singing
c. ??(that) John was singing
} occurred at noon.

That the value of *John* (or *the boy*) (see (10a)), in turn, belongs to a different ontological category than the value of *(that) John was singing* (see (10c)) is shown by the possibility of taking *John/the boy* – but not *(that) John was singing* – as the object argument of the transitive verb *kick* (see (11)).

(11) Mia kicked {
a. John/the boy
b. ??that John was singing
}.

The observation that *kick* only takes concrete physical arguments (which are located in a certain point in space; see Vendler, 1967b) then motivates the classification of the semantic values of *John* and *the boy* as an individual. The strategy from (10) and (11) has also been used to argue for a semantic category of facts (e.g. Ginzburg, 2005; Kastner, 2015; Vendler, 1967b), of propositions (Asher, 1993; Vendler, 1967a), of questions (Ginzburg, 1995; Grimshaw, 1979; Lahiri, 2002), and of kinds (Carlson, 1977; Chierchia, 1998; Landman, 2006).

It is important to point out that the success of this strategy stands and falls with the choice of the embedding predicate. Thus, selectionally super-flexible verbs like *remember* (which accept a wide range of different syntactic constructions; see Liefke, 2021) will indicate many fewer ontological distinctions (as is apparent from (12), which is acceptable for all of the object arguments in a–d).

(12) Mia remembers {
a. John/the boy
b. John's singing
c. that John was singing
d. whether John was singing
}.

That the success of this strategy also depends on the choice of the syntactic argument(!) is shown by the intuitive oddness of sentences like *Mia kicked a fly*.

Table 1 Proforms for entities from different semantic categories

Category	Pronoun	*wh*-word	Quantifier
individuals	*he, she, it*	*who, which, what*	*all, everything/-one*
events	*it*	*which, when, what*	*always, if*
worlds/situations	*will, would, then*	*? when*	*must, might, if*
times	*then, -ed* [past tense morpheme]	*when*	*always, daily, when(ever)*
locations	*there, it*	*where*	*everywhere, where(ever)*
propositions	*that, it*	*what*	*everything, what(ever)*
degrees	*yea, so*	*how (many/much)*	*more, -er*
manners	*(like) so*	*how*	*? like*
kinds	*so, such*	*how*	*all*

2.1.2 The Morphological Strategy: Proforms

An alternative – or complementary – strategy to the above capitalizes on so-called 'morphological category-specific items'. These items include quantifiers as well as proforms (paradigmatically, anaphoric pronouns and, on some accounts, *wh*-words). The morphological strategy assumes that natural languages lexicalize reference to different types of entities, such that different quantifiers and proforms refer to entities from distinct ontological categories. A selection of English pronouns, *wh*-words, and quantifiers is given in Table 1 (taken from Liefke, 2024b, 23; based on Rett, 2018, 5). This selection includes individual proforms (e.g. *he, she, it*), temporal proforms (e.g. tense markers), modal proforms (e.g. *will, would*), and propositional/sentential proforms (e.g. *that*).

Some of the items from Table 1 straightforwardly 'reveal' their referent's semantic category, as intended. This holds for those items that are exclusively associated with a single semantic category, like the English third-person pronouns *he* and *she*, and the degree demonstrative *yea* (see (13); Rett, 2015, 8). In particular, since *she* exclusively picks out individuals, it syntactically disambiguates (14) in favor of a 'DP + adjunct'-construction. (The complement of *see* on the alternative, gerundive analysis, viz. *a woman swimming*, can only be picked up by the pronoun *it*; cf. (1b).)

(13) Anna is *yea* tall. [accompanied by a gesture]

(14) Zeno saw [a woman]$_i$ swimming. *She*$_i$ was wearing a wetsuit.

The success of these examples notwithstanding, proforms and quantifiers are, in many cases, too unspecific to allow inference to a particular semantic category. In particular, many proforms refer to objects from intuitively distinct semantic categories (see the numerous occurrences of some proforms in Table 1). An example of such 'multi-categorial' morphological items is the singular neutral pronoun *it*. As is evidenced by (15), *it* can be used – among others – to refer to individuals (in (15a)), events (in (15b)), and propositions (see (15c)) (see Asher, 1993; Bach, 1986a; Krifka, 1990).

(15) a. Berta baked [a cake]$_i$. Anna ate it$_i$. (individual)

b. [The squeaking of the door]$_i$ caused Mia to cringe. It$_i$ made Noel's ears hurt. (event)

c. Ben believes [that figs are fruit]$_i$. Dana doubts it$_i$. (proposition)

In order to answer the co-classification challenge from (15) (multiple categorial reference) and (12) (selectional super-flexibility), Rett (2022) has proposed to distinguish semantic categories by considering the selection and reference behavior of ALL proforms, quantifiers, and predicates that are associated with a given semantic category, and by drawing category-distinctions on the basis of the most selective of these proforms, quantifiers, and predicates. Her proposed account would thus focus on the predicates *occur* and *kick* (see (10), (11)) and on the proforms *yea* and *she* (see (13), (14)), rather than on the expressions *remember* and *it*.

2.1.3 The Logical-Semantic Strategy: Quantificational Domains

To answer the semantic categorization problems that remain even in Rett's combined strategy, many researchers complement the strategies from Sections 2.1.1 and 2.1.2 with a strategy that focuses on the formal semantic modeling of the investigated language. This strategy is based on the observation that certain phenomena (paradigmatically: sentential entailments) can only be modeled if we assume an extra semantic domain whose elements are denoted by implicit (logical or semantic) arguments. The strategy is based on Quine's (1948) criterion of ontological commitment, according to which "to be is . . . to be the value of a variable" (32). It uses Davidson's (1977) observation that "ontology is forced into the open only where the theory finds quantificational structure" (251).

The logical-semantic strategy presupposes Montague's method of indirect interpretation, which obtains the semantic values of natural language expressions by interpreting these expressions' logical 'translations' in set-theoretic models (Montague, 1973; see Zimmermann, 2022).[4] The strategy starts from the logical formulas that serve as these translations. It identifies semantic commitments with the domains of existential quantifiers in these formulas.

An example of the logical-semantic strategy (due to Davidson, 1977) is given in (16)/(17). This example is based on the observation that capturing the intuitive entailments from (16) requires introducing an event variable, e (see (17)).[5]

(16) a. Brutus brutally stabbed Caesar on the forum.
⇒ b. Brutus brutally stabbed Caesar. (locative-PP drop)
⇒ c. Brutus stabbed Caesar. (adverb drop)

(17) a. $(\exists e)[\mathbf{stab}(e, \mathbf{brutus}, \mathbf{caesar}) \wedge \mathbf{brutal}(e) \wedge \mathbf{loc}(e) = \mathbf{forum}]$
b. $(\exists e)[\mathbf{stab}(e, \mathbf{brutus}, \mathbf{caesar}) \wedge \mathbf{brutal}(e)]$
c. $(\exists e)[\mathbf{stab}(e, \mathbf{brutus}, \mathbf{caesar})]$

The logical-semantic strategy has also been used to argue for a semantic category of possible worlds w (see (18a); Kratzer, 1991; Montague, 1970), times t (see (18b); Cariani, in press; Matthewson, 2006), kinds k (see (18c); Carlson, 1977; Landman, 2006), manners m (see (18d); Piñón, 2008; Schäfer, 2008), and degrees d (see (4a)/(5); Heim, 2000; Lassiter, 2012) – among others. In (18), $\rightsquigarrow$ is the translation function that sends natural language expressions (e.g. (16a)) to logical terms (here: (17a)). In (18c), $\leq$ is the instantiation relation between individuals and kinds.

(18) a. It may be raining in Bochum.
$\rightsquigarrow (\exists w)[\mathbf{rain}(w, \mathbf{bochum})]$
b. Ben called Mia (in c at @).
$\rightsquigarrow (\exists t)[t < t_c \wedge \mathbf{call}(@, t, \mathbf{ben}, \mathbf{mia})]$
c. Fred owns a rare dog.
$\rightsquigarrow (\exists x)[(\mathbf{dog}(x) \wedge \mathbf{own}(\mathbf{fred}, x)) \wedge (\exists k)[x \leq k \wedge \mathbf{rare}(k)]]$
d. John writes illegibly.
$\rightsquigarrow (\exists e)\left[\mathbf{write}(e, \mathbf{john}) \wedge (\exists m)[\mathbf{manner}(m, e) \wedge \mathbf{illegible}(m)]\right]$

We will see in the next section that Montague's semantic ontology relies heavily on the logical-semantic strategy.

---

4 For a step-by-step description of this method, the reader is referred to Liefke (2024b, 2.4.1).

5 In (17), **brutus** and **caesar** are individual constants that serve as the logical translations of the proper names *Brutus* and *Caesar*. **forum** is a location constant. **brutal** and **stab** are non-logical constants for properties of events and for individual-event relations, respectively. The nonlogical constant **loc** denotes a function from events to their location.

2.2 Montague's Semantic Ontology

Since Montague's semantics targets a small, well-defined subset of 1970s English (i.e. the PTQ-fragment) that has a fully specified ontology (see Montague, 1973), it is the perfect starting point for our investigation of semantic ontologies. Note that the PTQ-fragment excludes measure phrases, degree modifiers, and explicit comparatives alongside modifiers for kinds and interrogative expressions. As a result of the former, PTQ's ontology is similar to the ontology of 'degree-less' languages like Motu (see Section 1.1). As a result of the latter, PTQ's ontology lacks kinds and questions. Since some entailments of the form of (16) can be captured without reference to – or quantification over – events (see the account, in (19b), of the entailment from (19a)), Montague (1969) rejects a category of events (as does Montague, 1970, 1973).

(19) a. The sun rose at eight. $\Rightarrow$ The sun rose.

b. $\mathbf{rise}(\langle @, \mathbf{08{:}00}\rangle, \mathbf{sun}) \;\Rightarrow\; (\exists t)[\mathbf{rise}(\langle @, t\rangle, \mathbf{sun})]$

2.2.1 Montague's Extensional Ontology

To facilitate the type-theoretic analysis of the PTQ ontology (in Sections 4–5), I divide the PTQ-fragment into an extensional part (in Table 2) and an intensional part (in Table 3), following (Liefke, 2024b, section 3). These parts differ with respect to the substitutibility of their elements: While expressions from the extensional part allow the truth-preserving substitution of co-referential expressions (e.g. *Bill*, *the man*) and of truth-conditionally equivalent expressions (e.g. *Bill walks*, *The man walks*; see (20)), expressions from the intensional part are often taken to block this substitution (see (21)).

(20) a. [The man] walks.

b. The man is Bill.

$\Rightarrow$ c. [Bill] walks.

(21) a. Mary believes [that the man walks].

b. The man walks $\Leftrightarrow$ Bill walks

$\Rightarrow$ c. Mary believes [that Bill walks].

In virtue of its elements' substitutivity, the extensional part of the PTQ-fragment allows proper names to be interpreted as individuals (represented by properties of properties of individuals [= 'generalized quantifiers']) – rather than as individual concepts (or their representing properties of properties

Table 2 The extensional part of Montague's PTQ-fragment

pronouns:	$he_0, he_1, he_2, \ldots$	(individuals)
proper names:	*John, Mary, Bill*	(G[eneralized] Q's)
decl. sentences:	*John walks, . . .*	(truth-values)
common nouns:	*man, woman, park, fish, pen*	(properties of individuals)
intrans. verbs:	*run, walk, talk*	(properties of individuals)
transitive verbs:	*find, lose, eat, date, be*	(relations betw. individ'ls)
adverbs:	*rapidly, slowly*	(relations betw. properties)
determiners:	*a, the*	(property/GQ-relations)
quantifiers:	*every*	(property/GQ-relations)
prepositions:	*in*	(. . .)

of individual concepts).[6] Table 2 includes the expressions' semantic categories in the right-most column. In this column, 'GQ' is short for 'generalized quantifier'.

The fact that Table 2 contains individual proforms (viz. indexed versions of the pronoun *he*) already suggests that the PTQ-fragment carries a semantic commitment to individuals. While Montague's strategy of 'generalizing to the worst case'[7] (Partee, 1983, 34) prevents him from assuming individuals as the semantic values of referential determiner phrases (DPs), individuals play a central role in his interpretation of determiners and quantifiers (viz. as objects in the domain of existential and universal quantification; see (22)).

(22) a. A man walks. $\rightsquigarrow (\exists x)[\mathbf{man}(x) \wedge \mathbf{walk}(x)]$

b. Every man walks. $\rightsquigarrow (\forall x)[\mathbf{man}(x) \rightarrow \mathbf{walk}(x)]$

c. The man walks. $\rightsquigarrow (\exists x)(\forall y)[(\mathbf{man}(y) \leftrightarrow y = x) \wedge \mathbf{walk}(x)]$

Interestingly, in addition to individuals, Montague's ontology also contains points (or 'moments') of time. Since Montague further assumes that this domain is structured by a simple ordering, $\leq$ (Montague, 1973, 257–258; see Bach, 1986b, 577), PTQ's semantic ontology allows for a straightforward extension to tense and temporal expressions (along the lines described in [18b] and in Liefke, 2024b, 4.2.3).

[6] Parallel observations hold for the interpretation of nouns and intransitive verbs as properties of individuals (rather than as properties of individual concepts).

[7] This strategy interprets an expression as an object that is sufficiently complex to accommodate all uses of this expression (across different linguistic contexts) and all members of this expression's syntactic category.

Table 3 The intensional part of Montague's PTQ-fragment

decl. complements:	*that…, to…* [inf.]	(propositions)
sentence adverbs:	*necessarily*	(proposition/truth-value rel's)
intensional nouns:	*unicorn, price, temperature*	(p'ties of individual concepts)
intransitive verbs:	*rise, change*	(p'ties of individual concepts)
transitive verbs:	*seek* [= *try to find*]	(rel's to a centered proposition)
clause-taking Vs:	*believe, assert*	(rel's to a proposition)
control verbs:	*try, wish*	(rel's to a centered proposition)
adverbs:	*allegedly*	(relations between properties)
prepositions:	*about*	(…)

2.2.2 Montague's Intensional Ontology

To capture the substitution-resistance of predicates like *temperature* and *rise* (see (23)) and of the clausal complements of verbs like *believe* (see (21)), Montague's semantics interprets these expressions in terms of propositions and/or individual concepts (i.e. as properties of individual concepts, or as relations to a proposition; see the rightmost column in Table 3).

For reasons that will be detailed in Section 5, Montague analyzes propositions as characteristic functions of sets of ordered world/time pairs, or of sets of 'indices' (i.e. those indices at which the proposition is true). Individual concepts are identified with functions from indices to individuals. The interpretation of intensional nouns like *temperature* as properties of individual concepts blocks intuitively invalid inferences like (23) (Montague, 1973, 267–268; attributed to Barbara Partee).

(23) a. The temperature is ninety.
b. The temperature rises.
$\Rightarrow$ c. $^{??}$Ninety rises.

Since Montague's semantics prima facie does not quantify over indices, it might look like this semantics does not carry a commitment to indices (or to possible worlds). However, such quantification is covert in the modal box operator $\Box$ and in Montague's analysis of the intensional operators $^{\vee}$ (read: 'cup') and $^{\wedge}$ (read: 'cap'). The box operator, which is central to Montague's interpretation of the sentence adverb *necessarily*, is analyzed in terms of universal quantification over worlds (see (24); Muskens, 1995, 37).

(24) Necessarily $p \rightsquigarrow \Box\, p \quad (\equiv \forall w.\, p(w))$

The intensional operators, which are needed to switch from intensions to their actual-world extensions and vice versa, correspond to application to and abstraction from the implicit index parameter (see [25], where α is a well-formed expression and i is a fixed variable for the evaluation index).

(25) a. $^{\vee}\alpha = \alpha(i)$

b. $^{\wedge}\alpha = \lambda i.\alpha$

In view of the above, Montague's semantics for the PTQ-fragment assumes a rich descriptive ontology that includes individuals and individual concepts (see (22)/(23)), possible worlds and times (see (24)), propositions (see (21)), properties of individuals, properties of individual concepts, and generalized quantifiers, alongside objects of many other semantic categories.

I will show in Sections 4 and 5 how Montague reduces this ontology to a small subset of basic semantic categories (which has the same modeling scope as the descriptive ontology). However, before I do so, I sketch the most important extensions of Montague's ontology (in Section 2.3) and review the merits of typing the objects in these ontologies (in Section 3).

2.3 Larger Semantic Ontologies

I have already suggested (in Section 2.1) that most state-of-the-art semantics for extensions of the PTQ-fragment (e.g. Champollion, 2017; von Fintel & Heim, 2021) assume a substantially larger ontology than Montague's semantic ontology from Section 2.2. This is so since these extensions contain expressions (e.g. manner adverbs, measure phrases, plurals, mass nouns, and kind terms) whose behavior cannot be adequately modeled in Montague's ontology. We have already seen an instance of this strategy in (17) (which introduces events to capture entailments like (16)). Similar observations have motivated the assumption of events, manners, degrees, pluralities, substances, and kinds (see Figure 1 and the penultimate paragraph of Section 2.1.3). I will, at this point, not delve deeper into the arguments for each of these categories (see instead Liefke, 2024b, section 4). Rather, I will content myself with listing the most frequently discussed categories and (some of) their more prominent proponents (in Table 4).

Admittedly, the different focus of the semantic theories whose objects are listed in Table 4 gives rise to partly different semantic ontologies. For example, since Champollion's (2017) semantics of distributivity, aspect, and measurement is not concerned with modeling interrogatives or attitude reports, its

Table 4 Extensions of Montague's ontology (overview)

events	(Davidson, 2001; Parsons, 1990; Vendler, 1967b)
manners	(Dik, 1975; Piñón, 2008; Schäfer, 2008)
situations	(Barwise & Perry, 1983; Ginzburg, 2005; Kratzer, 1989)
questions	(Ginzburg, 1995; Hamblin, 1976; Groenendijk & Stokhof, 1984)
intervals	(Champollion, 2017; Partee, 1973; Rooij & Schulz, 2014)
degrees	(Heim, 2000; Lassiter, 2012; von Stechow, 1984)
kinds	(Carlson, 1977; Chierchia, 1998; Landman, 2006)
pluralities	(Champollion & Brasoveanu, 2022; Link, 1983)
vectors	(Winter, 2005; Zwarts, 1997; Zwarts & Winter, 2000)
content individuals	(Bondarenko, 2020; Kratzer, 2006; Moulton, 2009)
⋮	⋮

ontology – plausibly[8] – does not carry a commitment to questions or content individuals (in contrast to, e.g., Hamblin, 1976 or Kratzer, 2006).

The resulting pluralism notwithstanding, the ontologies of contemporary semantic theories converge to a surprising extent. This holds at least as soon as these theories consider larger – phenomenally more diverse – fragments of the target language (that cover a wide[r] range of phenomena), or as soon as these theories are identified with the sum of different semantics for different classes of phenomena. Independently of these considerations, many semantic theories already share a substantial part of their ontological commitments (e.g. to individuals, worlds/situations, properties, propositions, and generalized quantifiers). Quite a few contemporary semantic theories – including semantics for manner adverbs (see (18d); Schäfer, 2008), semantics for distributivity (see Figure 1; Champollion, 2017), and semantics for attitude reports (see Kratzer, 2006) – further share the assumption of events.

My intermittent sketch of semantics for these phenomena has already suggested that the members of different ontological semantic categories are related in interesting ways (see also my introduction to this Element). This holds, for example, for propositions and possible worlds (at which propositions are true

[8] This is motivated by Ockham's principle of ontological parsimony, according to which ontological categories should only be adopted if the semantic phenomena that they are intended to explain resist an explanation through those categories that are assumed anyway (see also Section 3.3).

or false), for properties and individuals (see (22)), for questions and propositions (which serve as answers to questions), and for manners and events (see [18d]).

The following sections capture these relations with the help of the Simple Theory of Types (see Church, 1940). The latter is a bookkeeping system that allows one to keep track of different semantic categories (see Muskens, 2011). A key merit of type systems lies in their providing a hierarchical structure: Rather than merely assigning objects to semantic categories (as was already done in Section 2), type systems distinguish between basic (or 'primitive') and complex (or 'derived') objects. Of these objects, the former resist a decomposition into simpler objects (and, as a result, carry ontological commitment). Objects of a complex type are constructed from basic – or less complex – objects through special type-forming rules (e.g. function space formation).

To show how the typing of semantic objects is achieved, I first introduce a number of different type systems, starting with a system for Montague's extensional ontology, TY_1, and with Gallin's streamlined version, TY_2, of Montague's (1970) *Intensional Logic* IL (in Sections 4–5). Following TY_2's extension to larger linguistic fragments (in Section 6), I will then discuss arguments for reducing – and for unifying – types (in Section 7). I precede my introduction of different type systems by reviewing the merits of typing the objects in a language's semantic ontology:.

3 Merits of Typing Ontologies

3.1 Compositionality

I have already noted at the beginning of Section 1 that the compositional computation of semantic values requires identifying (type-)relations between the objects from different semantic categories. To see why this is the case, consider the example in (26):

(26) Matti is sleeping.

Intuitively, we want to say that (26) is true if the referent of *Matti*, that is, ⟦Matti⟧, has the property of sleeping. However, in the absence of a deeper connection between individuals and properties, we will not be able to obtain the semantic value of (26) from ⟦Matti⟧ and ⟦sleep⟧ (or ⟦is sleeping⟧) alone. This holds in particular so long as we have not specified the semantic linking operation + in the compositional analysis, ⟦Matti⟧ + ⟦sleep⟧, of ⟦Matti is sleeping⟧.

The type-logical analysis of properties (⟦sleep⟧) solves this problem: By analyzing properties as functions from individuals to truth-values (or to propositions), this analysis straightforwardly accounts for the compositional interpretation of (26) (in (27)).

(27) $[\![\text{sleep}]\!]\,([\![\text{Matti}]\!])$

Specifically, this account analyzes the semantic value, $[\![\text{sleep}]\!]$, of *sleep* as a function, $x \mapsto [\![x \text{ sleeps}]\!]$, from individuals x to the truth-value $[\![x \text{ sleeps}]\!]$ (or equivalently, as a characteristic function of the set, $\{x : [\![x \text{ sleeps}]\!] = \mathbf{1}\}$, of sleeping individuals). The application of this function to the individual $[\![\text{Matti}]\!]$ then yields the truth-value **1** [= 'true'] (or **0** [= 'false']).

3.2 Type Checking and Type Inference

The typing of semantic objects enforces a rigorous type checking on the outputs of the compositional interpretation. This checking is enabled by the type-driven nature of the semantic interpretation process (see, e.g., Heim & Kratzer, 1998, chapter 3.1; Zimmermann & Sternefeld, 2013; based on Klein & Sag, 1985). Type-driven interpretation is a general procedure for the provision of semantic values that obtains these values from the semantic values of syntactically simple expressions (e.g. lexical elements, words) together with information about the syntactic structure of the interpreted complex expression. It assumes that the semantic values of syntactically complex expressions are obtained from the values of their immediate syntactic constituents through the familiar composition rules (paradigmatically: forward or backward functional application, FA; see Charlow & Bumford, 2025, section 1.1).

Specifically, type-driven interpretation assumes an interpretation relation, $[\![\cdot]\!]$ (or translation relation, $\rightsquigarrow$), between analyzed syntactic structures (that is, LFs) and (logical terms for) the objects in our TY_n model structures.[9] This relation is governed by a 'base rule', (T0), which specifies the interpretation of lexical elements. The remaining rules specify how the interpretation of complex syntactic structures depends on the interpretation of their constituents. The two most elementary such rules, (T1) and (T2), are given next:

(T0) If X is a word and $\boldsymbol{A}$ its interpretation, then $[\![X]\!] = \boldsymbol{A}$.

(T1) If $[\![X]\!] = \boldsymbol{A}$, then a structure, $[X]$, that contains X as its only constituent is interpreted as follows: $[\![[X]]\!] = \boldsymbol{A}$.

(T2) If $[\![X]\!] = \boldsymbol{A}$ and $[\![Y]\!] = \boldsymbol{B}$, then if $\boldsymbol{A}(\boldsymbol{B})$ is well-typed, $[\![[XY]]\!] = \boldsymbol{A}(\boldsymbol{B})$; if $\boldsymbol{B}(\boldsymbol{A})$ is well-typed, $[\![[XY]]\!] = \boldsymbol{B}(\boldsymbol{A})$.

For example, given that $[\![\text{sleep}]\!]([\![\text{Matti}]\!])$ is well-typed, rule (T2) yields the interpretation of *Matti sleeps* from the interpretations, $[\![\text{Matti}]\!]$ and $[\![\text{sleep}]\!]$, of the proper name *Matti* and the intransitive verb *sleep*. Since type-driven interpretation allows interpretations to be "shuffled around as long as the result

[9] Type-driven interpretation that proceeds via the method of indirect interpretation is sometimes called *type-driven translation* (see Klein & Sag, 1985). The method of indirect interpretation is described in the prequel Element, *Natural Language Ontology and Semantic Theory* (Liefke, 2024b).

is a structure in which all the parts fit together appropriately" (Rothstein, 2012, 239) it has sometimes been called 'shake-and-bake semantics' (Bach, 1980).

Type-driven interpretation contrasts with Montague's (1970, 1973) 'rule-by-rule approach' to semantics (the label goes back to Bach, 1977). This approach assumes that, for each syntactic rule that describes the formation of complex linguistic expressions, there is a corresponding semantic rule. Semantic rules describe how a semantic object (i.e. a member of a given semantic domain) is obtained from the semantic values of the expression's constituents. Type-driven interpretation differs from the rule-by-rule approach in requiring a much smaller set of semantic/interpretation rules: Since it views semantic rules as dependent on syntactic rules, the rule-by-rule approach demands that same-domain objects that interpret the results of applying different syntactic rules (e.g. *walk rapidly* [IAV + IV] and *try to walk* [IV//IV + IV]) are also obtained through different semantic rules.[10] In contrast, type-driven interpretation effectively combines multiple such rules (for *walk rapidly, try to walk*: in the rule (T2)).

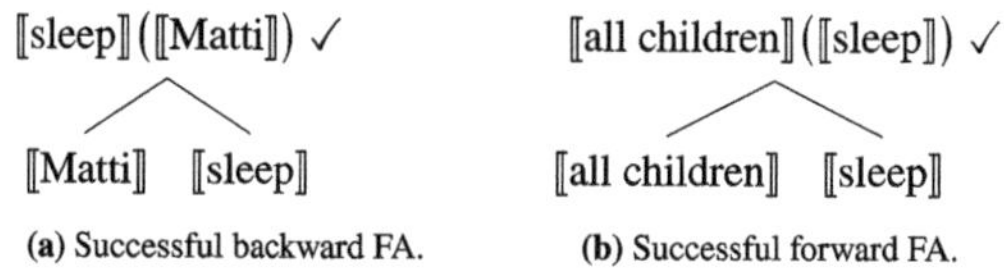

Figure 2 Successful cases of functional application.

Assuming type-driven interpretation, one can explain the meaningful- or meaninglessness of complex expressions with respect to whether the semantic value of these expressions results from a seamless application of composition rules (e.g. (T2)). Such seamless application is evidenced by the semantic values of *Matti is sleeping* (i.e. (26)) and *All children are sleeping*. These values each result from different instances of Functional Application (FA): The semantic value ⟦Matti is sleeping⟧ is obtained by applying the value of the sentence's predicate, that is, *sleep*, to the value of the sentence's subject, *Matti* (i.e. $[\![X]\!] + [\![Y]\!] = [\![Y]\!]([\![X]\!])$; see Figure 2a). In contrast, since quantifier phrases like *all children* are typically taken to denote (a characteristic function of) a set of properties – rather than an individual –, the semantic value ⟦All children are sleeping⟧ is obtained by applying the value of the sentence's subject, that is, *all children*, to the value of the sentence's predicate, *sleep* (i.e. $[\![X]\!] + [\![Y]\!] = [\![X]\!]([\![Y]\!])$; see Figure 2b).

[10] Following (Montague, 1970), IV stands for 'intransitive verb' (e.g. *walk*). IV//IV and IAV stand for 'infinitive-complement verbs' (e.g. *try to*) and for 'verb phrase adverb' (e.g. *rapidly*).

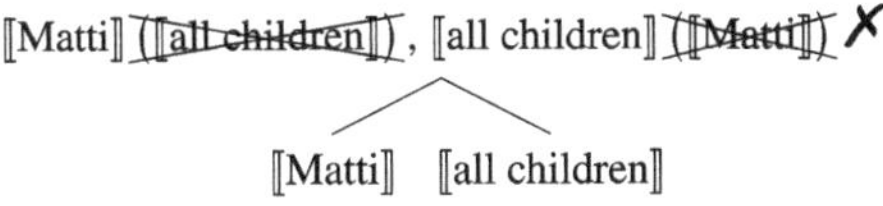

Figure 3 An unsuccessful case of functional application.

These assumptions about the semantic composition of intuitively meaningful expressions also help reverse engineer the semantic category of a given expression from the categories of its mother and its sister constituents (i.e. it facilitates type inferences; see Gunter, 1992). Thus, from the semantic categories of ⟦Matti⟧ (i.e. 'individual') and ⟦Matti is sleeping⟧ (i.e. 'truth-value'), we can infer the category of ⟦sleep⟧. The latter is the category of functions from objects of the sister category (above: individuals) to objects of the mother category (above: truth-values) (Gutzmann, 2019, 46–49; Winter, 2016, 59–61). I will return to this kind of type inferences in Section 4.

Note that, since type-driven interpretation starts at the level of linguistic expressions, it can also be used to provide a semantic explanation of grammaticality and syntactic well-formedness. Accordingly, a complex expression is grammatical if the semantic values of its constituents at all levels of syntactic structure (i.e. clauses, phrases, and words) combine through the familiar composition rules. The fact that this is the case in Figures 2a and 2b then explains the grammaticality of the sentences *Matti is sleeping* and *All children are sleeping*.

Inversely to the above, type-driven interpretation also accounts for the ungrammaticality and meaninglessness of certain other complex expressions. This meaninglessness results from the inability to combine the semantic values of these expressions' constituents at some level of syntactic structure through the usual composition rules. In this way, the meaninglessness of the complex expression (28) can be explained through the impossibility to combine the individual ⟦Matti⟧ with the generalized quantifier ⟦all children⟧ through FA (see Figure 3). This impossibility, in turn, explains the observation that *Matti all children* does not form a grammatical sentence and cannot serve as a constituent in a larger, more complex expression.

(28) Matti all children

Arguably, these demands on 'matching types' also classify some expressions as deviant that are intuitively both grammatical and meaningful. These include the sentences in (29a) and (30a), which are subject to type-clashes (see (29c), (30c)). To solve this problem, most contemporary semantic theories adopt additional composition rules (e.g. Predicate Modification [PM]; see Heim & Kratzer, 1998, 65) and introduce a small set of dedicated type-shifting operations (e.g. the Montague Rule [LIFT], Argument Lowering, Value Raising; see Hendriks, 1993, 2020; Partee, 1987). The need for further composition rules is exemplified by (29a) (due to Charlow & Bumford, 2025), which requires PM to combine the properties that serve as the semantic values of *happy* and *cat* (see the boldfaced material in (29b)).

(29) a. The happy cat is purring.
b. (⟦the⟧(**⟦happy⟧ ∩ ⟦cat⟧**))(⟦pur⟧)
c. ⟦happy⟧ ~~(⟦cat⟧)~~, ⟦cat⟧ ~~(⟦happy⟧)~~

The need for type-shifting operations is exemplified by (30a). This sentence requires that ⟦Matti⟧ is shifted to the semantic type of ⟦all other children⟧, that is, the type for generalized quantifiers (see (30c)). It is achieved through Partee's (1987) type-shifter LIFT $:= \lambda x.\, \{P : P(x)\}$ (based on Montague, 1970), which sends individuals to the set of their properties (see (30b)).

(30) a. Matti and all other children are sleeping.
b. ((⟦and⟧(⟦all other children⟧))(**LIFT(⟦Matti⟧)**))(⟦sleep⟧)
c. (⟦and⟧(⟦all other children⟧)) ~~(⟦Matti⟧)~~

One may worry that this remedy overshoots its aim, resulting in an unwelcome 'rescue strategy' for a large number of intuitively meaning*less* expressions. While this worry is not unfounded (see the possibility of 'salvaging' (28) by sending ⟦Matti⟧ to a generalized quantifier through LIFT and combining the result with ⟦all children⟧ through PM), the small number of composition rules (see Charlow, 2014; Section 1 of this Element) and the strong restrictions on admissible type-shifts (e.g. injectivity, lambda-definability, permutation-invariance; see van Benthem, 1991; Zimmermann, 2020) impose strict limits on this strategy for the resolution of type-clashes.[11]

3.3 Parsimony

We have already seen that type theory distinguishes between basic (or ontologically primitive) and complex (or ontologically derived) objects. Since complex objects are constructed from basic objects through the iterated application of special type-forming rules (see below), type-theoretic ontologies need not commit – at least not in the same way – to all of their elements. Rather, their

[11] The alternative possibility to salvage (28) by representing ⟦Matti⟧ as the property 'be Matti' (i.e. $\{x : x = ⟦\text{Matti}⟧\}$) is blocked by the fact that some theories do not assume an 'individual-to-property' type-shifter. This fact reflects the observation that some languages (e.g. Mandarin, ASL) lack the copula *be* and/or predicative uses of proper names.

commitments are reduced to elements of a basic type, alongside the specific operations (e.g. function-space formation, set formation) that derive elements of a complex type from elements of a more basic type. The commitment to function-space and/or set formation brings with it a commitment to abstract objects like functions and sets (see Quine, 1948).

Consider the extensional ontology of Montague's PTQ-fragment (see Section 2.2.1). By Montague's assignment of basic types, only individuals (i.e. the referents of proper names and pronouns) and truth-values (i.e. the extensions of declarative sentences) are entities of a basic type. On the level of type-forming operations, related observations hold for set formation or, more generally, for function-space formation. From individuals and truth-values, these operations enable the formation of (characteristic functions of) sets of individuals or, equivalently, of functions from individuals to truth-values (see Section 4). Once these entities and operations are available, the remaining objects of Montague's extensional ontology come 'for free': In particular, if we assume that properties of individuals are adequately represented (or coded) by sets of individuals, Montague's parsimonious type system straightforwardly provides properties. The same holds for propositions (if we assume a basic type for possible worlds and the possibility of adequately representing propositions as sets of possible worlds).

Importantly, the use of type theory to reduce a semantic theory's ontological commitments obeys the principle of ontological parsimony (more commonly known as *Ockham's razor*). This principle demands that the number of entities or ontological categories that a specific theory assumes should not be increased beyond necessity – in Ockham's original formulation, "Entiae non sunt multiplicanda praeter necessitatem" (Clauberg, 2009, 320). Applied to the ontology of natural language semantics, Ockham's principle demands that ontological categories should only be adopted if the semantic phenomena that they are intended to explain (see, e.g., the phenomena in Section 2.1) resist an explanation through those categories that are assumed anyway. I will show in Section 6 that this reasoning can – perhaps surprisingly – be used to argue *for* the assumption of primitive events and kinds.

In the history of analytic philosophy, Ockham's principle has famously been used to argue against a commitment to properties (or universals). In particular, class nominalists hold that the 'one over many' problem – which demands an account of the multiple instantiation of properties (e.g. the exemplification of redness by Ed Sheeran's hair, the red pen on my desk, and all British double-decker buses) – has a simple solution in terms of class membership: If properties are construed as classes, multiple instantiation is simply membership in the same class (e.g. in the class {Ed Sheeran's hair, my red pen, UK

Bus-1, UK Bus-2, . . .}; see Armstrong, 1980, 28–43; Lewis, 1983). Replacing classes by sets (or their characteristic functions) straightforwardly yields the Montagovian – extensional – picture of properties.

3.4 The Meaning/Reference-Relation

Beyond this, typing objects makes explicit the meaning/reference-relation. This holds at least so long as non-referential meanings are understood as Carnapian intensions, that is, as functions from possible worlds to the expressions' extensions at these worlds (see Carnap, 1988). On Montague's Carnapian ontology, the intensions of declarative sentences (i.e. propositions) are functions from possible worlds (or indices) to the propositions' truth-value at these worlds. The intensions of common nouns and intransitive verbs (i.e. properties) are functions from possible worlds to the sets of individuals that exemplify the property at these worlds (see (25)).

Since Montague's ontology identifies the extensions of an expression with the range of the function that serves as the expression's intension (for sentences: truth-values; for common nouns: sets of individuals), it directly encodes the relation between meaning and reference. Specifically, the intension, f, of an expression determines the expression's extension, that is, $f(w)$, for each evaluation world w. Inversely, since Montague identifies functions with their courses-of-values, the extensions, x_w, of an expression for each world jointly determine the expressions' intension as that function f such that, for each w, $f(w) = x_w$ (Zimmermann, 2017, 193–194; see Ben-Avi & Winter, 2007; de Groote & Kanazawa, 2013).

The described relation between intensions and extensions is reminiscent of the relation between Frege's (1997) notions of sense [*Sinn*] and reference [*Bedeutung*]. In particular, by determining the referent (or truth-conditional contribution) of a given expression at the relevant world, Carnapian intensions emulate the semantic function of Fregean senses (see Burge, 2005). Montague's type label for possible worlds, that is, s, is explicitly chosen to pay reverence to Frege's notion of *Sinn* (Zimmermann, 2022, 340). To capture the Fregean spirit of Montague's ontology – as well as of its particular type-theoretic implementation (Church, 1951; see Section 5) – this ontology is sometimes called the 'Frege-Church ontology' (Kaplan, 1976; see Liefke, 2024a).

Importantly, a type-theoretic encoding of the meaning/reference-relation is evidenced by *all* intensional ontologies that construe meanings as functions from some evaluation index to referents (as pointed out in Muskens, 2005). These include the ontologies of Kratzer-style situation semantics (Bondarenko, 2022; Kratzer, 2002), of impossible-world semantics (Barwise, 1997; Rantala, 1982; Zalta, 1997), of truthmaker semantics (Liefke, 2020; Moltmann, 2020), and of semantics with more complex evaluation indices (Plummer & Pollard, 2012; Pollard, 2015). The meaning/reference-relation is even encoded in the semantic ontology of some hyperintensional theories (see e.g. Muskens, 2005; Thomason, 1980): While these theories treat non-referential meanings as hyperintensions (for declarative sentences: as semantically primitive propositions; see Sections 6.1.2, 6.2.2), they still assume Carnap-style intensions and extensions. The meaning/reference-relation is then made available by a mapping from hyperintensions to intensions. For example, this mapping sends primitive propositions to sets of possible worlds. Since hyperintensional theories construct the hyperintensions of other expressions as functions to primitive propositions, this mapping generalizes to the hyperintensional meanings of all expressions.

4 Type Theory Basics

With arguments for semantic typing in place, I now introduce some type systems that have been used to 'tame' the semantic ontologies from Section 2. For ease of exposition, I first discuss the type-theoretic regimentation of Montague's extensional ontology from Section 2.2.1 (in the present section). Following a discussion of different ways of obtaining intensions, I then present a type-theoretic regimentation of Montague's intensional ontology from Section 2.2.2 (in Section 5).

4.1 Types and Rules of TY_1

I have already pointed out that type systems distinguish between basic and complex types. To capture the ontology of the extensional part of the PTQ-fragment, Montague (1973) assumes two basic types, that is, individuals (type e) and truth-values (type t). From these types, the types of all other extensional objects are obtained through the rule of function-space formation (i.e. **Rule 1**; see Church, 1940). This rule establishes that the type for functions from objects of one type to objects of another type is itself a type:[12]

Rule 1 (Function-space formation). If α and β are types, then $\langle \alpha, \beta \rangle$ is a type, where $\langle \alpha, \beta \rangle$ is the type for functions from objects of type α to objects of type β.

A single application of **Rule 1** to the types e and t yields (among others) the type for functions from individuals to truth-values, $\langle e, t \rangle$, and the type for functions from truth-values to truth-values, $\langle t, t \rangle$. Objects of type $\langle e, t \rangle$

[12] To emphasize that this rule is also available for the formation of intensional and other types, I do not further specify 'type' in this rule.

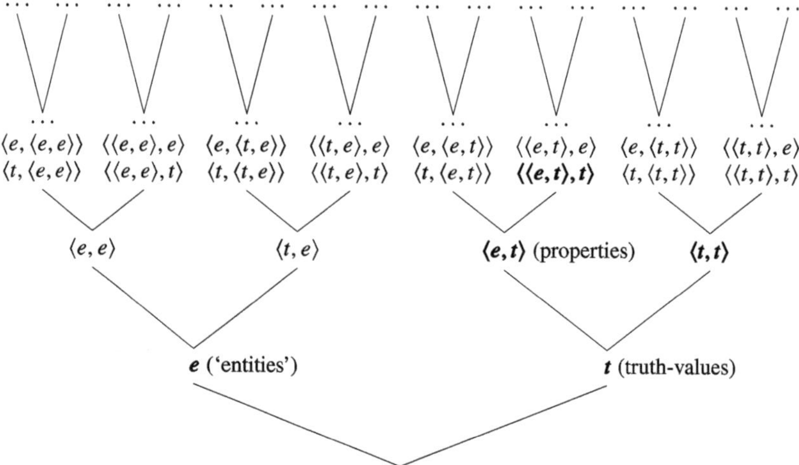

Figure 4 The hierarchy of extensional (TY_1) types.

are characteristic functions of sets of individuals (i.e. extensional properties) that serve as the extensions of common nouns and intransitive verbs. Objects of type $\langle t,t\rangle$ are characteristic functions of sets of truth-values that serve as the extensions of unary sentential operators (paradigmatically, of sentential negation).

A second application of function-space formation (to types $\langle e,t\rangle$ and t) yields the type for (characteristic functions of) sets of extensional properties, $\langle\langle e,t\rangle,t\rangle$. Objects of this type (i.e. extensional generalized quantifiers) serve as the extensions of determiner and quantifier phrases. The simplest types that are obtained from e and t through **Rule 1** are given in Figure 4. In this figure, the previously discussed types are marked in boldface.

One may expect that some expressions from Montague's PTQ-fragment are interpreted as n-ary functions or relations, rather than as unary functions (as is enforced by **Rule 1**). This holds, for example, for sentential conjunction (i.e. *and*) as well as for transitive verbs like *find*: Intuitively, *and* denotes a function that sends ordered *pairs* of truth-values [= the extension of each of the two conjuncts] to a single truth-value [= the extension of the conjunctive sentence] (see Figure 5a). The verb *find* denotes a relation between individuals, or a relation between a generalized quantifier and an individual.

To accommodate this interpretation, one could extend **Rule 1** to the formation of n-ary functional and/or relational types (along the line of Muskens, 1995). However, there is a straightforward procedure for turning multiary functions into unary functions of a higher type (Winter, 2016, 57–59). This procedure, called 'Currying' (after Haskell Curry, 1961) or 'Schönfinkelization' (after Moses Schönfinkel, 1924; see Heim & Kratzer, 1998, 30–31), works by

$[\![\text{and}]\!]^2([\![\text{Sam works}]\!], [\![\text{Matti sleeps}]\!])$

$[\![\text{and}]\!]^2$ $[\![\text{Sam works}]\!]$ $[\![\text{Matti sleeps}]\!]$

(a) Binary semantics for conjunction.

$([\![\text{and}]\!]^1([\![\text{Matti sleeps}]\!]))([\![\text{Sam works}]\!])$

$[\![\text{Sam works}]\!]$ $[\![\text{and}]\!]^1([\![\text{Matti sleeps}]\!])$

$[\![\text{and}]\!]^1$ $[\![\text{Matti sleeps}]\!]$

(b) Unary semantics for conjunction.

Figure 5 Binary versus unary semantics for conjunction.

feeding the function its arguments one by one in inverse order, beginning with the last element of the ordered n-tuple (see (31)). In (31), $x_1, \ldots, x_n$ are arguments of the types $\alpha_1, \ldots, \alpha_n$. f is a function that sends ordered n-tuples of objects of types $\alpha_1, \ldots, \alpha_n$ to truth-values:

(31) $\textsc{curry}(f) = \lambda x_n \ldots \lambda x_1 . f(x_1, \ldots, x_n)$

Specifically, CURRY modifies the 'binary' interpretation of *and* from Figure 5a (see [32a]) into the unary function in (32b). This unary function is used in the interpretation in Figure 5b.

(32) a. $[\![\text{and}]\!]^2 = \lambda\langle p, q\rangle . p \wedge q$

b. $[\![\text{and}]\!]^1 = \textsc{curry}([\![\text{and}]\!]^2) = \lambda q \lambda p . p \wedge q$

Remark that there is nothing wrong in principle with including n-ary functions and relations in one's semantic ontology. In particular, the addition or deletion of n-ary functions does not affect the theory's adequacy. However, since much of contemporary syntax assumes binary-branching structures of the form in (32b) (see Figure 5b) – and since the restriction to unary functional types is in line with (Montague, 1970, 1973) and with much contemporary work – I will hereafter assume only unary functional types (next to basic types). An overview of the types of objects in Montague's extensional ontology is given in Table 5.

Note that these objects and functions already supply many of the relations that serve to categorize objects in large, state-of-the-art ontologies (e.g. the ontology for Chemical Entities of Biological Interest, ChEBI; see Degtyarenko et al., 2008).[13] These include 'is a property of' (type-$\langle e, t\rangle$), 'is a binary relation between' (type-$\langle e, \langle e, t\rangle\rangle$), 'is an n-ary relation between' (type-$\langle e, \langle \ldots, \langle e, t\rangle\rangle\rangle$), and 'is a relatum of'.

I have stated above that Montague's extensional ontology contains objects of two basic types (or *sorts*), that is, individuals and truth-values. Following

[13] This ontology is available at `www.ebi.ac.uk/chebi`.

Table 5 Types in Montague's extensional ontology

Expression	Object	Type
–	individuals	e ('entity')
declarative sentences	truth-values	t
sentential negation	sets of truth-values	$\langle t, t\rangle$
sentential conjunction	functions to sets of truth-values	$\langle t, \langle t, t\rangle\rangle$
nouns, intransitive verbs	(fcts of) sets of individuals	$\langle e, t\rangle$
DPs, quantifier phrases	extensional gen'zd quantifiers	$\langle\langle e, t\rangle, t\rangle$
transitive verbs	functions to sets of individuals	$\langle\langle\langle e, t\rangle, t\rangle, \langle e, t\rangle\rangle$
adverbs	functions to sets of individuals	$\langle\langle e, t\rangle, \langle e, t\rangle\rangle$
determiners/quantifiers	fcts to generalized quantifiers	$\langle\langle e, t\rangle, \langle\langle e, t\rangle, t\rangle\rangle$
prepositions	...	...

Gallin's (1975) convention of subscripting a type theory's name by the number of its basic types – not counting the truth-value type t – this type system is called 'TY_1' (for *one-sorted type theory*).[14] For completeness, the definition of TY_1 types is given next:

Definition 1 (TY_1 types). The set of TY_1 types is the smallest set such that

(i) e and t are TY_1 types;
(ii) if α and β are TY_1 types, then $\langle\alpha, \beta\rangle$ is a TY_1 type. **(Rule 1)**

This completes my introduction of Montague's extensional/TY_1 types. I will move to a restriction and intensional extension of these types and their associated objects in Sections 4.3 and 5. However, before I do so, I first show how TY_1 types give rise to the type checking mechanism that has been discussed in Section 3.2.

4.2 Type Checking in TY_1

As expected, TY_1 straightforwardly explains the semantic acceptability (or meaningfulness) of complex expressions. To help identify type matches or mismatches, Figure 6 enriches the semantic trees from Figure 3 with the types of each of their nodes. This enrichment is reminiscent of type judgments in

[14] Accordingly, TY_n is a theory with $n + 1$ basic types. TY_0 (with the basic type t) is Henkin's (1963) theory of propositional types; TY_2 (with the basic types e, s, and t) is Gallin's (1975) streamlined variant of Montague's (1970) intensional logic, IL (see Section 5.2). For a list of type systems with more than three basic types, the reader is referred to Table 9 (in Section 6.2.3).

$[\![\text{sleep}]\!]([\![\text{Matti}]\!]) : t$ ✓

$[\![\text{Matti}]\!] : e \quad [\![\text{sleep}]\!] : \langle e,t\rangle$

(a) Successful backward FA (typed).

$[\![\text{all children}]\!]([\![\text{sleep}]\!]) : t$ ✓

$[\![\text{all children}]\!] : \langle\langle e,t\rangle,t\rangle \quad [\![\text{sleep}]\!] : \langle e,t\rangle$

(b) Successful forward FA (typed).

Figure 6 Successful cases of functional application, with typing.

$[\![\text{sleep}]\!]([\![\text{all children}]\!]) : t$ ✓

$[\![\text{all children}]\!] : \langle\langle e,t\rangle,t\rangle \quad [\![\text{sleep}]\!] : \langle\langle\langle e,t\rangle,t\rangle,t\rangle$

Figure 7 Alternative to the interpretation in Figure 6b, with typing.

modern type theories (see Martin-Löf, 1975) and has recently been adopted in type-theoretically conscious applications of formal semantics (see e.g. Elliott, 2017; Moulton, 2015; Winter, 2016, chapter 3).

In particular, the type-enrichment of Figure 2a (in Figure 6a) identifies the semantic value of *sleep* with a (type-$\langle e,t\rangle$) function from individuals to truth-values. Since it identifies $[\![\text{Matti}]\!]$ with a suitable argument of this function (i.e. a type-e individual), it straightforwardly explains the semantic acceptability of (26). Similar observations hold for the sentence *All children are sleeping* (see Figure 2b; in Figure 6b): since Figure 6b identifies $[\![\text{all children}]\!]$ with a generalized quantifier, that is, with a function from type-$\langle e,t\rangle$ functions to truth-values (which takes as input arguments of the type of $[\![\text{sleep}]\!]$), it straightforwardly explains the semantic acceptability of the sentence *All children are sleeping*.

Notably, assuming that $[\![\text{all children}]\!]$ is a generalized quantifier, one could also obtain the type-t interpretation of *All children are sleeping* by treating $[\![\text{sleep}]\!]$ as a function from generalized quantifiers to truth-values (i.e. as an object of type $\langle\langle\langle e,t\rangle,t\rangle,t\rangle$; see Figure 7). This treatment is assumed in Groenendijk and Stokhof (1989) (see Hendriks, 1993), where it is implemented through the operation of Argument Raising. In contrast to the interpretation of *All children are sleeping* from Figure 6b, the treatment from Figure 7 enables the sentence's compositional interpretation through backward FA, analogous to Figure 6a. However, the typing from Figure 6b is preferred to the typing from Figure 7 on grounds of simplicity (reflected in a preference for lower-rank types).

Considerations like these can also be used to explain the semantic deviance of constructions like *Matti all children* (see Figure 8): since the semantic value of *Matti* does not have the right type to serve as an argument of the function that is denoted by *all children* (and vice versa), the two expressions cannot compose in the expected way.

⟦Matti⟧~~(⟦all children⟧)~~, ⟦all children⟧~~(⟦Matti⟧)~~ ✗

⟦Matti⟧ : e ⟦all children⟧ : $\langle\langle e, t\rangle, t\rangle$

Figure 8 An unsuccessful case of functional application, with typing.

4.3 From TY_1 Types to Extensional Types

I have suggested in the context of Figure 4 that not all TY_1 types are associated with objects in Montague's extensional ontology. In particular, while Montague's semantics for the PTQ-fragment assumes type-e individuals (see Table 4), it does not assume extensional functions *to* individuals (e.g. type $\langle e, e\rangle$ or $\langle t, e\rangle$). Instead, all complex objects in Montague's extensional ontology are functions to truth-values (i.e. characteristic functions of sets).

The restriction of functional types to types that "end in t" (Groenendijk & Stokhof, 1990, 5) is owed to the semantic identification of non-referential expressions with their truth-conditional contribution (following Davidson, 1967). It is further motivated by the observation (due to Partee & Rooth, 1983) that characteristic functions facilitate the modeling of semantic phenomena like entailment and coordination (see Keenan & Faltz, 1985). Following Partee and Rooth (1983), entailment – or, more generally, semantic inclusion – is defined as the functional counterpart of set-theoretic inclusion: for two linguistic expressions A and B, it thus holds that $A \Rightarrow B$ (read: 'A includes B') iff, for all x, if $[\![A]\!](x) = \mathbf{1}$, then $[\![B]\!](x) = \mathbf{1}$. In the semantics literature, types whose objects allow for this treatment are called *conjoinable* (Partee & Rooth, 1983), *relational* (Groenendijk & Stokhof, 1990), or *Boolean* (Kac, 1992; Winter, 2002). The set of these types is defined as follows:

Definition 2 (Boolean types). A type τ is Boolean iff

(i) $\tau = t$ or
(ii) $\tau = \langle\alpha, \beta\rangle$, where β is a Boolean type.

Using the notion of Boolean type, one can restrict TY_1 types to those types that more accurately reflect the commitment of the extensional part of Montague's PTQ-fragment:

Definition 3 (extensional types). The set of extensional types is a proper subset of the set of TY_1 types such that

(i) e and t are extensional types;
(ii) if α and β are TY_1 types and β is a Boolean type, then $\langle\alpha, \beta\rangle$ is an extensional type.

This definition includes all types from Table 4. To capture the semantic commitments of the full PTQ-fragment, I will extend the set of extensional types to intensional types in Section 5.

5 Typing Montague's Ontology

I have already argued (in Section 2.2.2) that the intensional part of Montague's PTQ-fragment uses quantification and abstraction over possible worlds (i.e. objects of type s) and that Montague treats intensions as functions from possible worlds to the expressions' extensions at these worlds (see Carnap, 1988). As a result, the intensions of declarative sentences are objects of type $\langle s,t\rangle$ (i.e. propositions). The intensions of common nouns and extensional intransitive verbs (e.g. *man*, *walk*) are functions from possible worlds to characteristic functions of sets of individuals (type $\langle s,\langle e,t\rangle\rangle$). The intensions of intensional nouns and intensional intransitive verbs [ITVs] (e.g. *temperature*, *rise*) are functions from worlds to characteristic functions of sets of individual concepts (type $\langle s,\langle\langle s,e\rangle,t\rangle\rangle$). A more comprehensive list of intensional PTQ-types is given Table 6.

All of this shows that Montague's intensional ontology explicitly uses possible worlds in the metatheory. However, different ontologies for the PTQ-fragment assume different ways of obtaining intensional objects (and attendantly, intensional types). In what follows, I present three competing ways of forming intensional types (i.e. Gallin, 1975 vs. Montague, 1970 vs. Montague, 1974) and survey their respective advantages and drawbacks. I close this section by identifying the relation between the intensional objects that are obtained in these different ways.

Table 6 Types in Montague's (1970) intensional ontology

Expression	**Object**	**Type (IL/TY$_2$)**
declarative sentences	propositions	$\langle s,t\rangle$
sentence adverbs	functions to propositions	$\langle\langle s,t\rangle,\langle s,t\rangle\rangle$
extens'l nouns, IVs	properties of individuals	$\langle s,\langle e,t\rangle\rangle$
intens'l nouns, ITVs	p'ties of indiv'l concepts	$\langle s,\langle\langle s,e\rangle,t\rangle\rangle$, or $\langle\langle s,e\rangle,t\rangle$
determiner phrases	intensional GQs	$\langle s,\langle\langle s,\langle e,t\rangle\rangle,t\rangle\rangle$
determiners/quant's	fcts to intensional GQs	$\langle\langle\langle s,e\rangle,t\rangle,\langle s,\langle\langle s,\langle e,t\rangle\rangle,t\rangle\rangle\rangle$
extens'l transitive Vs	GQ-to-property functions	$\langle\langle s,\langle\langle s,\langle e,t\rangle\rangle,t\rangle\rangle,\langle s\langle e,t\rangle\rangle\rangle$
clause-taking verbs	propos'n-to-property fcts	$\langle\langle s,t\rangle,\langle s,\langle e,t\rangle\rangle\rangle$
control verbs, adv's	property-to-property fcts	$\langle\langle s,\langle e,t\rangle\rangle,\langle s,\langle e,t\rangle\rangle\rangle$
prepositions	...	...

5.1 Intensional Ontology without Fully-Fledged Worlds

To obtain the types and objects from Table 6, Montague's Intensional Logic (IL) extends the set of TY_1 types via a rule for the formation of intensional types. This rule (i.e. **Rule 2**) assumes that the type for functions from possible worlds, or indices, to objects of some type α is also a type (Montague, 1970, 227–228; 1973, 256).

Rule 2 (Intensional type-formation). If α is a type, then $\langle s, \alpha \rangle$ is a type.

The resulting set of types is specified immediately below:

Definition 4 (IL types). The set of IL types is the smallest set such that

(i) e and t are IL types; (basic TY_1 types)

(ii) if α and β are IL types, then $\langle \alpha, \beta \rangle$ is an IL type; (**Rule 1**)

(iii) if α is an IL type, then $\langle s, \alpha \rangle$ is an IL type. (**Rule 2**)

Note that **Definition 4** does not assume a basic type for possible worlds (or indices). Instead, it introduces possible worlds only indirectly, that is, through the new **Rule 2**. The introduction of worlds through an additional type-forming rule has a key merit: It reduces the number of predicted, but ontologically irrelevant types. The addition of this rule thus serves a similar purpose as the restriction of β to a Boolean type in the definition of extensional types (see **Definition 3**). It has long been assumed that the lack of a basic type for possible worlds also accounts for the absence of pronouns for possible worlds (see von Fintel & Heim, 2021, 13). However, following Stone (1997), more recent work has assumed modal or possible-world proforms (see Section 2.1.2, Table 1).

5.2 Intensional Ontology with Fully-Fledged Worlds

The lack of a fully-fledged type for possible worlds requires that quantification and abstraction over worlds be achieved through dedicated operators (i.e. through the operators $\Box$, $\Diamond$, and $^\wedge$). Gallin's (1975) streamlined version of Montague's type system, TY_2 (for *two-sorted type theory*), compensates for this challenge by adopting a fully-fledged type for possible worlds. (The name for this type system, TY_2, already suggests that this system assumes an additional basic type next to the basic TY_1 types e and t.) The set of TY_2 types is specified next:

Definition 5 (TY_2 types). The set of TY_2 types is the smallest set such that

(i) e, s, and t are TY_2 types; (basic TY_1 types + s)

(ii) if α and β are TY_2 types, then $\langle\alpha,\beta\rangle$ is an IL type. **(Rule 1)**

In Definition 5, the assumption of a basic type for possible worlds obviates the adoption of an intensional type-forming rule like **Rule 2**: the iterated application of **Rule 1** to the basic TY_2 types already yields all the intensional types from Table 6. In fact, the set of TY_2 types contains many types that are irrelevant for the semantics of the PTQ-fragment (see Zimmermann, 2023). These include most complex types that 'end in s or e' (an exception being the type for individual concepts; see Section 2.2.2). An example of such ontologically irrelevant types is the type $\langle t,s\rangle$ (i.e. functions from truth-values to possible worlds).

5.3 Intensional Ontology with Propositional Functions

It is sometimes argued that even the fairly parsimonious ontology of IL already contains many more intensional objects than are required to capture the semantics of English (details in Kaplan, 1976; Zimmermann, 2023; see Section 2.2.2). This is evidenced by the ontologies from Montague (1974) and Cresswell (1973), which restrict intensions to Russell (1996)-style propositional functions. The latter are objects of type $\langle\alpha_1,\langle\ldots\langle\alpha_n,\langle s,t\rangle\rangle\rangle\rangle$, where $\alpha_1,\ldots,\alpha_n$ are Russellian types[15] (defined in what follows). To emphasize that Russellian propositions are, in principle, neutral with respect to the analysis of intensions (s.t. they can be identified with more finely grained objects than sets of possible worlds; see Sections 3.4 and 6.1.2), I call the type for Russellian propositions 'p' (for *propositions*). Russellian types are defined as follows:

Definition 6 (Russellian types). The set of Russellian types is the smallest set such that

(i) e and p are Russellian types;

(ii) if α and β are Russellian types, then $\langle\alpha,\beta\rangle$ is a Russellian type. **(Rule 1)**

Because of their Russellian origin, propositional function-based ontologies like these are sometimes called 'Russellian ontologies' (Kaplan, 1976; see Liefke, 2024a).

[15] Since propositions are commonly identified with zero-place propositional functions, propositional functions include propositions.

Items (34) and (35) contrast a Russellian ontology (b.) with a Frege–Church ontology (a.) for the compositional interpretations of (23b) and (33). To emphasize the ontological categories in this interpretation, I have annotated the compositional semantic values in (34) and (35)–(36) with their (IL or Russellian) types:

(33) Bert believes that the woman is smart.

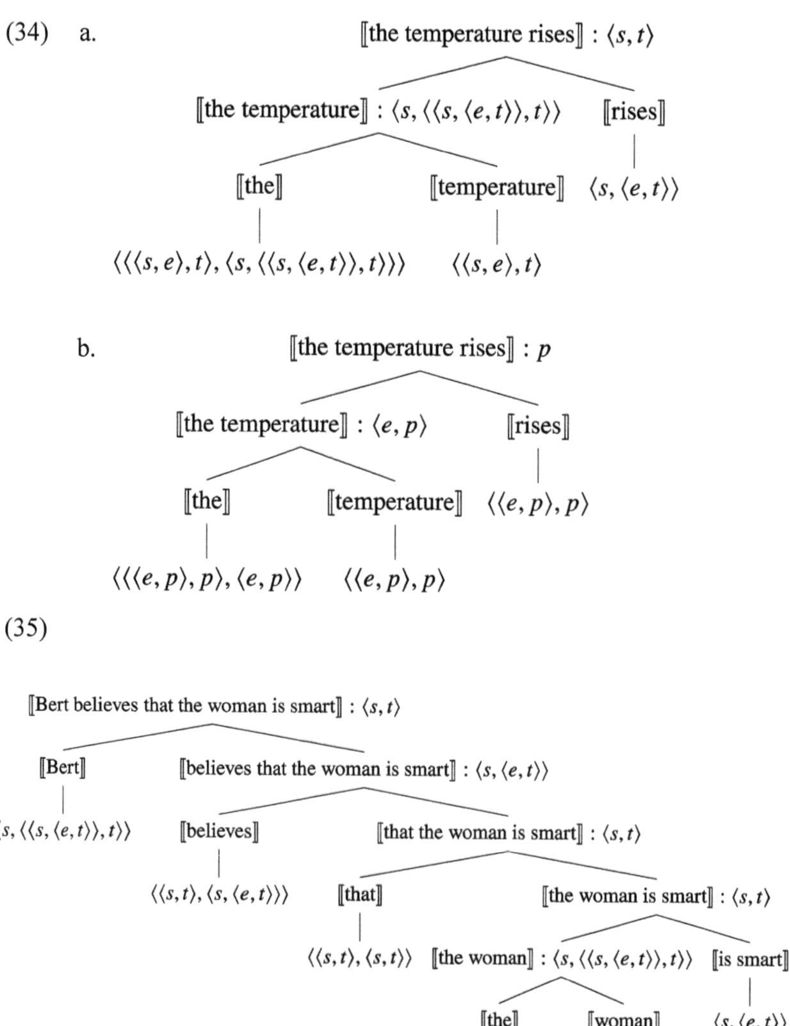

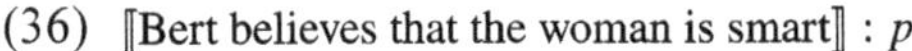
(36) ⟦Bert believes that the woman is smart⟧ : p

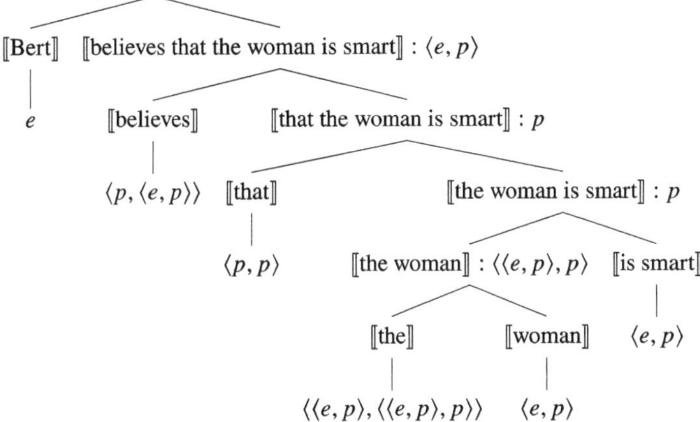

The Russellian interpretation in (34b) implements Kaplan's proposal to replace individual concepts (type $\langle s, e\rangle$) with one-place propositional functions (i.e. type-$\langle e,p\rangle$; see Section 2.2.2). Kaplan's account further suggests that intensional nouns like *temperature* and intensional transitive verbs like *rise* receive an interpretation in the type $\langle\langle e,p\rangle,p\rangle$ (i.e. as second-order propositional functions). The Russellian and the Frege-Church ontology of the PTQ-fragment are contrasted in Table 7.[16]

Table 7 shows how different semantics for the same natural language fragment can share little to no ontological assumptions: Assume for the purpose of exposition that Russellian propositions (type p) are not analyzed as sets of possible worlds (type $\langle s, t\rangle$). Then, by Ritchie's (2016) Principle of Carrying Commitments (see Section 1.1), the Frege-Church and the Russellian ontology have nothing in common. This holds at least for the level of the object theory, which contains the semantic values of linguistic expressions.[17] In particular, while the simplest [= least-complex type] objects in the Russellian ontology are individuals (type e – due to its adoption of a 'simplest types first'[18] strategy;

[16] For a detailed discussion of the relation between the Russellian and the Frege–Church ontology, the reader is referred to Liefke (2024a) and Zimmermann (2023).

[17] The occurrence of e as an 'ingredient' in both Russellian and IL types already suggests that Russellian and Frege-Church ontologies share at least some meta-theoretical assumptions (see Section 7).

[18] This strategy assumes that some subcategories (e.g. referential DPs) may allow for an interpretation as a simpler, less complex object (e.g. as an individual; see Hendriks, 1993, 2020).

Table 7 Intensional types in a Frege-Church and a Russellian ontology

Expression	Frege-Church (IL/TY$_2$)	Russellian Type
proper names	$\langle s, \langle\langle s, \langle e, t\rangle\rangle, t\rangle\rangle$	e
declarative sentences	$\boldsymbol{\langle s, t\rangle}$	p
modal/sentence adverbs	$\langle\langle s, t\rangle, \langle s, t\rangle\rangle$	$\langle p, p\rangle$
nouns, IVs	$\boldsymbol{\langle\langle s, e\rangle, t\rangle}$	$\langle\langle e, p\rangle, p\rangle$
determiner phrases	$\langle s, \langle\langle s, \langle e, t\rangle\rangle, t\rangle\rangle$	$\langle e, p\rangle$
determiners/quantifiers	$\langle\langle\langle s, e\rangle, t\rangle, \langle s, \langle\langle s, \langle e, t\rangle\rangle, t\rangle\rangle\rangle$	$\langle\langle\langle e, p\rangle, p\rangle, \langle e, p\rangle\rangle$
extensional transitive Vs	$\langle\langle s, \langle\langle s, \langle e, t\rangle\rangle, t\rangle\rangle, \langle s, \langle e, t\rangle\rangle\rangle$	$\langle e, \langle e, p\rangle\rangle$
clause-taking verbs	$\langle\langle s, t\rangle, \langle s, \langle e, t\rangle\rangle\rangle$	$\langle p, \langle e, p\rangle\rangle$
control verbs, adverbs	$\langle\langle s, \langle e, t\rangle\rangle, \langle s, \langle e, t\rangle\rangle\rangle$	$\langle\langle e, p\rangle, \langle e, p\rangle\rangle$

see Partee, 1992, 115) and Russellian propositions (type p), the basic semantic objects in Montague's IL-ontology are Frege-Church propositions (type $\langle s, t\rangle$) and properties (type $\langle s, \langle e, t\rangle\rangle$). I have printed these objects/types in boldface in Table 7.

The above suggests that different ontologies for the same language or fragment have different motivations. For the 'competition' between Russellian and Frege-Church (or TY$_2$) ontologies, this is indeed the case: while the Russellian ontology contains the simplest objects – individuals (type e) are intuitively less complex than functions from possible worlds to sets of individuals (type $\langle s, \langle e, t\rangle\rangle$) –, only the ontology of TY$_2$ contains the referents of modal proforms. The ontology of Montague's IL lies in between these two extremes. Since TY$_2$ allows for overt quantification and abstraction over possible worlds, the rest of this Element will use TY$_2$. However, the reader should not identify this methodological move with an indication of the author's preferred ontology.

6 Typing Larger Ontologies

I have argued in Section 2.3 that, to widen the scope of Montague's intensional semantics, one needs to extend the number of entities or types in one's semantic ontology. The most principled strategy for such an extension lies in identifying these entities with objects of a complex TY$_2$ (or some other readily available) type. This strategy has been adopted for the semantic treatment of questions (which are commonly analyzed as sets of propositions; see Section 6.1.1) and manners (which have been analyzed as sets of events; see Section 6.1.3). However, in a significant number of cases, such treatment is not straightforwardly possible. This is already acknowledged by Bach (1986b, 582), who observes that "As . . . new things come in [to our semantic model-structures,] it is reasonable to want to put a little more structure into our domains." In what follows, I identify some reasons for introducing such additional structure (in Section 6.2). These include efforts to generalize existing basic types to include 'new' types, or to merge different types into a broader, uniform type (in Section 6.3).

6.1 Strategy 1: Exploit Complex Types

6.1.1 Questions

Historically, one of the first extensions of the PTQ-fragment has been to interrogatives (e.g. (37a); see Groenendijk & Stokhof, 1984; Hamblin, 1976b; Hausser & Zaefferer, 1978; Karttunen, 1977). In particular, Hamblin (1976) identifies the semantic values of interrogatives, that is, questions, with the set of all atomic propositions that count as possible answers to the question (see (37b)). Karttunen (1977) analyzes questions as the set of the question's true answers relative to the evaluation index. Assuming the familiar possible worlds-analysis of propositions, both of these accounts treat questions as objects of type $\langle\langle s,t\rangle,t\rangle$.

(37) *Background:* There are only three individuals, that is, Matti, Noah, and Oskar

a. Who is sleeping?

b. {'Matti is sleeping', 'Noah is sleeping', 'Oskar is sleeping'}

To specify what counts as a 'possible answer' to a question, newer semantics for interrogatives (e.g. Ciardelli et al., 2018; Theiler et al., 2018; Uegaki, 2019) replace Hamblin's notion of a possible answer with the notion of a piece of information that resolves the issue raised by the question. These semantics analyze questions as *downward-closed* sets of propositions. The downward closure of these sets is supported by the observation that if a piece of information p resolves the issue raised by a given question Q, any stronger piece of information q (s.t. $q \subset p$) will also resolve the issue raised by Q. The effect of replacing sets of propositions (see (37b)) by downward-closed sets is illustrated in (38).

(38) {'No one is sleeping', 'Someone is sleeping',
'Matti is sleeping', 'Noah is sleeping', 'Oskar is sleeping',
'Matti and Noah are sleeping', 'Matti and Oskar are sleeping',
'Noah and Oskar are sleeping', 'Matti, Noah, and Oskar are all sleeping'}

The interpretation of interrogatives as downward-closed sets of propositions also captures the intuitive entailment relations between more and less specific questions (see (39)):

(39) a. Who is sleeping and snoring?
$\rightsquigarrow \lambda p.\, p \subseteq \{w : \exists x.\, x \text{ snores and sleeps in } w\}$

$\Rightarrow$ b. Who is sleeping?
$\rightsquigarrow \lambda p.\, p \subseteq \{w : \exists x.\, x \text{ sleeps in } w\}$

At a compositional level, the analysis of questions as objects of type $\langle\langle s,t\rangle,t\rangle$ enables the interpretation of question words (e.g. *who*) and interrogative-embedding predicates (e.g. *wonder*) as objects of TY_2 types. These objects are identified with functions from properties to questions (type $\langle\langle s,\langle e,t\rangle\rangle, \langle\langle s,t\rangle,t\rangle\rangle$) and with functions from questions to properties of individuals (type $\langle\langle\langle s,t\rangle,t\rangle, \langle s,\langle e,t\rangle\rangle\rangle$), respectively.

6.1.2 Possible Worlds and Situations

In an effort to capture the relation between propositions and truth-at-a-world (see Section 3.4), some hyperintensional theories (e.g. Fox, Lappin, & Pollard, 2002; Pollard, 2008) analyze possible worlds as ultrafilters on propositions (type $\langle p,t\rangle$, where p is the type for primitive propositions; see Section 3.4, 6.2.2). These theories combine the introduction of a new type of entity (here: primitive propositions) with the use of a new complex type that is constructed from TY_2 types and this new type. They assume that propositions are elements of a Boolean algebra, B_p. The latter is an algebraic structure that is ordered by a reflexive transitive relation, $\sqsubseteq$, that has a top element, $\top$, and a bottom element, $\bot$. Ultrafilters on propositions are then (i) upwards-closed and (ii) meet-closed proper subsets of B_p (iii) that contain, for each proposition p, either p or its complement (see Pollard, 2008, 263).

In virtue of (i), it holds that, if a proposition p, is in this set and $p \sqsubset q$, then q is also in this set. In virtue of (ii), it holds that, if two propositions, p and q, are in this set, their meet, $p \sqcap q$, is also in this set. Proposition (iii) demands that, for each proposition p, either p or its complement, p', is in this set. The concept of an ultrafilter is graphically illustrated in the Hasse diagram in Figure 9a. There, the ultrafilter is the set of all grey nodes.

Interestingly, the analysis of possible worlds as sets of propositions inverses the relation between propositions and worlds. In Montague's semantics, a proposition [= set of possible worlds] p is true at a world w iff w is a set-theoretic element of p (see (40a)). Inversely, in Pollard's semantics, a primitive

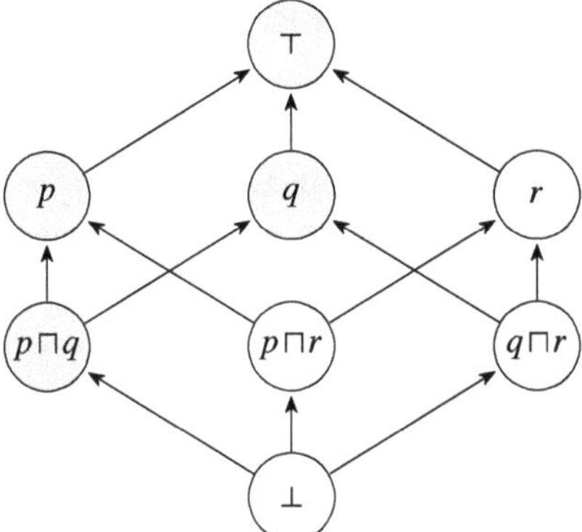

(a) The **possible world** in which only 'Matti is sleeping' (p) and 'Noah is sleeping' (q) are true.

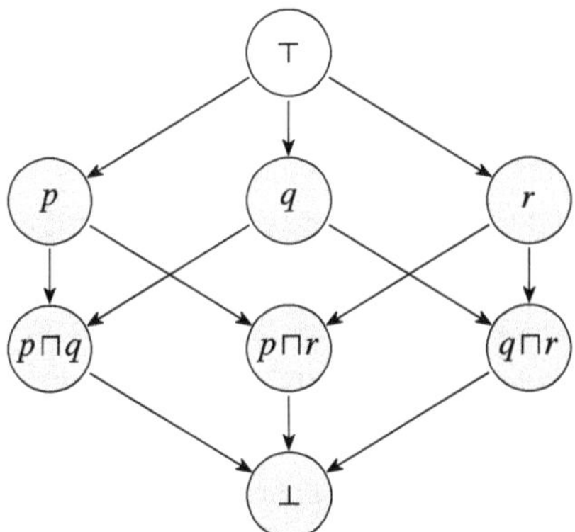

(b) A hyperintensional analysis of the **question** 'Who is sleeping?', i.e. $\{p : p \sqsubseteq \text{'s.o. is sleeping'}\}$.

Figure 9 Type-$\langle p, t\rangle$ representations of possible worlds (a) and questions (b).

proposition p is true at a possible world [= set of propositions] w iff p is a set-theoretic element of w (see (40b), where $\chi(w)$ is the characteristic function of the ultrafilter w).

(40) a. Montague (1973): 'p is true at w' iff $w \in p$ (or $p(w) = \mathbf{1}$)

b. Pollard (2008): 'p is true at w' iff $p \in w$ (or $(\chi(w))(p) = \mathbf{1}$)

Note that Pollard's semantics analyzes possible worlds as objects of the same type as hyperintensional questions (see Figure 9b, based on (39b)). However, a Pollard-style hyperintensional semantics is still able to distinguish worlds from questions. This is due to the fact that the type-$\langle p, t\rangle$ representations of worlds and questions have different properties (i.e. being an [upward-closed] ultrafilter resp. being a downward-closed set). It is further due to the possibility of defining subtypes by predicates for their properties (for details, see Pollard, 2008, 276–277). Analogous considerations hold for type-$\langle p,t\rangle$ representations of situations (i.e. spatio-temporal world parts; see Kratzer, 1989), which use prime filters of propositions (Liefke, 2017).

Since prime filters do not require that, for each proposition p, B_p contains either p or its complement, they straightforwardly capture the partiality of situations. The possibility of representing situations by prime filters even extends to informationally partial situations (see Liefke & Werning, 2018). The latter are spatio-temporal world-parts that may be informationally incomplete (e.g. such that they only contain *some* of their inhabitants' properties). Informationally partial situations are hence what Perry (1986) has called 'aspects' of a world.

To provide non-referential meanings of names and pronouns that avoid overt reference to possible worlds, Kaplan (1976) has proposed to represent individual concepts by (type-$\langle e, \langle s,t\rangle\rangle$) propositional functions (see my Sections 2.2.2, 5.3). This representation is preserved in a hyperintensional version of Kaplan's approach that interprets proper names and pronouns as objects of type $\langle e,p\rangle$.

Arguably, one could 'de-hyperintensionalize' Pollard's semantics by replacing primitive propositions with sets of possible worlds. The resulting account would analyze indices (classically, possible worlds) as complex entities of type $\langle\langle s,t\rangle,t\rangle$ (i.e. as generalized quantifiers over primitive worlds). While this account is equivalent (up to coding/typing) to a model of Montague's IL, the surjective relation between p and $\langle s,t\rangle$ (s.t. different primitive propositions may be associated with the same set of possible worlds; see Thomason, 1980) – and the resulting many-to-one relation between ultrafilters on propositions and generalized quantifiers over worlds – suggests that IL models of a given natural language fragment reduce to Pollard's account. For a detailed discussion of this reduction, the reader is referred to Liefke (2017).

6.1.3 Manners

To avoid an excessive proliferation of basic types, Umbach, Hinterwimmer, and Gust (2022) have proposed to analyze manners as similarity classes of events (i.e. as objects of type $\langle v,t\rangle$, where v is the type for events; see Umbach & Gust, 2014, 325–329). Such objects are sets of events that are indistinguishable with respect to a contextual parameter that includes the relevant dimensions of comparison. In the analysis of the manner m from (41), this parameter is called $\mathcal{F}$; SIM is a similarity relation that compares two events (i.e. its first and second argument) relative to this parameter (its third arguments).

(41) $(\exists e)\big[\mathbf{manner}(m,e) \leftrightarrow m = \{e' : \textsc{sim}(e',e,\mathcal{F})\}\big]$

For the 'John writing' example from (18d)/(42a), the dimensions in this parameter include, for example, proficiency level (beginner, advanced), style (handwritten, typed), and neatness (orderly, messy; see Umbach & Gust, 2014). The manner *m* in the interpretation of (18d)/(42a), i.e. (42b), is then analyzed as the set of events that resemble John's writing in at least one of these parameters (presumably in their messiness and attendant illegibility; see Umbach et al., 2022, 327–328).

(42) a. John writes illegibly.

$\rightsquigarrow$ b. $(\exists e)\big[\textbf{write}(e, \textbf{john}) \wedge (\exists m)[\overbrace{m = \{e' : \textsc{sim}(e', e, \mathcal{F})\}}^{m \text{ is a manner of } e} \wedge \textbf{illegible}(m)]\big]$

The analysis of manners as sets of events helps capture intuitive entailments between embedded manner *how*-clauses and bare infinitives or gerundive small clauses (see Liefke, 2023b):

(43) a. Mary saw John write(ing) the letter.
[≡ Mary (visually) witnessed the event of John's writing the letter.]

$\Rightarrow$ b. Mary saw how [≡ in which manner] John wrote the letter.

In particular, the entailment in (43) is supported by the observation that Mary cannot witness John's writing of the letter without also witnessing (or noting) the particular way in which John is writing the letter. Attendantly, every scenario that makes (43a) true will also make (43b) true. I will argue in Section 7 that cross-categorial entailments like (43) provide important support for the unification of types/semantic categories.

For reasons of space, I refrain from providing a detailed discussion of other semantic categories whose objects have been analyzed through a complex TY_2 (or related) type. A selection of these categories is given in Table 8.

6.2 Strategy 2: Proliferate Basic Types

My discussion from the previous subsection already suggests two key reasons for introducing new basic [= non-derived] types, namely: facilitating day-to-day semantics and providing more finely grained objects. I discuss both of these reasons next.

6.2.1 Merit (i): Easy Day-to-Day Semantics

I have shown in Section 6.1.2 that same-type representations of intuitively different objects (e.g. worlds and questions) can be distinguished as definable subtypes. This distinguishability notwithstanding, it is often convenient to refer to these subtypes [or *sorts*] directly (i.e. through the use of different type labels). This holds, for example, for the type-$\langle\langle p,t\rangle,\langle e,p\rangle\rangle$ interpretation of verbs like

Table 8 Complex-type reductions of 'new' objects

Category	Type	Analysis	Representation	Source
individual concepts	$\langle s,e\rangle$	$\langle e,\langle s,t\rangle\rangle$	propositional fcts	(Kaplan, 1976)
		$\langle e,p\rangle$	hyperintensional propositional functions	(Liefke, 2017)
properties		$\langle e,t\rangle$	sets of individuals	(Montague, 1973)
		$\langle e,p\rangle$	propositional functions	(Chierchia, 1984)
kinds,	k	$\langle e,t\rangle$	sets of individuals	(Link, 1983)
groups	g	$\langle e,t\rangle$	sets of individuals	(Bennett, 1975)
worlds	s	$\langle p,t\rangle$	ultra-filters on propositions	(Pollard, 2008b)
situations	s	$\langle p,t\rangle$	prime filters on proposit's	(Liefke, 2017)
questions	q	$\langle\langle s,t\rangle,t\rangle$	sets of alternatives	(Hamblin, 1976)
		$\langle p,t\rangle$	sets of basic propositions	(Pollard, 2008a)
degrees	d	$\langle e,t\rangle$	classes of individuals	(Cresswell, 1976)
[modal ~]		$\langle\langle s,t\rangle,t\rangle$	sets of propositions	(Portner, 2016)
manners	m	$\langle v,t\rangle$	similarity classes of events	(Umbach, 2022)
intervals	i	$\langle v,t\rangle$	equivalence classes of events	(Rooij & Schulz, 2014)

wonder, which intuitively only accept as arguments type-$\langle p,t\rangle$ representations of questions, but not representations of possible worlds. The introduction of a designated (sub)type for questions, q – and attendant interpretation of *wonder* in the type $\langle q,\langle e,p\rangle\rangle$ – straightforwardly solves this challenge. Similar observations hold for the assumption of different type-e subtypes for kinds, degrees, and content individuals (see Section 6.3.1) and for different type-s subtypes for situations and events (see Section 6.3.2).

6.2.2 Merit (ii): Granularity

The introduction of new basic types is further supported by the ability to provide more finely-grained identity-conditions for intensional objects. This support only applies to types that are associated with *non-decomposable* primitive objects.[19] Paradigm examples of this support include arguments for the

[19] As a result, this support does not apply to the TY_2 analyses of questions and manners.

adoption of primitive propositions (see e.g. Chierchia, 1984; Pollard, 2008; Thomason, 1980). These arguments start from the observation that Montague's semantics identifies the semantic values of all declarative sentences that have the same truth-value at all possible worlds (or indices; see Section 2.2.2). Specifically, since sentences (44a) and (44b) are both true at all worlds, they are interpreted as the same Montague-style proposition, namely, as the set of all possible worlds, W:

(44) a. Everything is self-identical.

b. $1^3 + 12^3 = 9^3 + 10^3$.

Since Montague's semantics assumes that the value of an attitude report is compositionally computed from the semantic values of its constituents, it falsely infers the agent's logical omniscience from their knowledge of a single necessarily true proposition (see (45); based on Hintikka, 1975).

(45) a. $[\![\text{Cleo knows that everything is self-identical}]\!]^{@}$
$= \textbf{know}\big(@, \textbf{cleo}, \{w : \text{everything is self-identical in } w\}\big)$ (T)

b. $\{w : \text{everything is self-identical in } w\}$
$= \{w : 1^3 + 12^3 = 9^3 + 10^3 \text{ in } w\} \quad = W$

$\not\Rightarrow$ c. $[\![\text{Cleo knows that } 1^3 + 12^3 = 9^3 + 10^3]\!]^{@}$
$= \textbf{know}\big(@, \textbf{cleo}, \{w : 1^3 + 12^3 = 9^3 + 10^3 \text{ in } w\}\big)$ (F)

The replacement of sets of possible worlds by primitive propositions (type p) as the intensions of declarative sentences – and the attendant distinction between the semantic values of (44a) and (44b) – blocks this inference.

Replacing sets of possible worlds with primitive propositions also helps gain more finely-grained semantic values for predicate expressions. This replacement even blocks inferences like (46) (based on Pollard, 2008) that are still valid in situation semantics (Kratzer, 1989, 2002): Since each individual that is a groundhog in some situation is also a woodchuck in this situation, situation semantics cannot distinguish between the semantic values of the *that*-clauses in (46a) and (46b).

(46) a. Bill believes that Punxsutawney Phil is a groundhog. (T)

b. In all possible worlds/situations, all groundhogs are woodchucks.

$\not\Rightarrow$ c. Bill believes that Punxsutawney Phil is a woodchuck. (F)

Similar arguments have been used to support the introduction of primitive individual concepts (see Pollard, 2008), primitive degrees (see Champollion, 2017, 31–32; following Cartwright, 1975; Parsons, 1970), and primitive manners (see Alexeyenko, 2015; Dik, 1975; Piñón, 2007; Schäfer, 2008). Note, however, that the referenced accounts vary with respect to whether they treat these objects as belonging to a new basic type or to a new sort (within an established basic type; see Section 6.3).

Its merits notwithstanding, the described increase in granularity comes at a price: the inability to capture intuitively *valid* inferences like the one in (47). This inability is due to the fact that primitive objects lack natural [= non-stipulated] identity-conditions. Consequently, if one assumes that propositions have very strict (or no) identity-conditions, one is unable to account for the intuitive validity of (47).

(47) a. Tom thinks that Bob borrowed a book from Alice.

$\Rightarrow$ b. Tom thinks that Alice lent a book to Bob.

Inversely, if one assumes that propositions have sufficiently loose identity-conditions (allowing one to capture (47)), one runs the risk of falsely predicting the validity of inferences like (45) and (46).

6.2.3 Overview of Natural Language Type Systems

A selection of type systems that result from extending Gallin's type system TY_2 from Section 5.2 with new basic types is given in Table 9. Note that the majority of these systems have not actually been labeled 'TY_n' (for $n \in \mathbb{N}$). Rather, I have added these labels for integration with Gallin's naming convention for type systems (see Muskens, 1995). In the semantics literature, 'TY_n' is sometimes alternatively written 'Ty_n' (Beaver, 2001), 'Ty n' (Zimmermann, 1985, 2022), or 'Ty-n' (Rett, 2022). In Table 9, 'AHS' stands for Pollard's (2008, 2015) Agnostic Hyperintensional Semantics.[20]

Of the type systems from Table 9, some take the type s to also include spatio-temporal parts of possible worlds (i.e. situations; Barwise, 1981; Kratzer, 1989). This holds, for example, for the type systems from Muskens (2005) and from Liefke and Werning (2018) (based on Liefke, 2014). Since some propositions may be neither true nor false at a situation, they require the introduction of a third truth-value (or rather, truth-*combination*), **N** (read: 'neither true nor false'). The combination **N** is needed, for example, for the evaluation of (26) at a situation in which the proper name *Matti* does not have a referent.

[20] Pollard calls this semantics 'agnostic' since it leaves open "the question of whether propositions are sets of worlds or worlds are (maximal consistent) sets of propositions" (Pollard, 2015, 535).

Table 9 Different type systems for natural language semantics

Name	Basic types	Source
TY_0	t	(Henkin, 1963)
TY_1	t, e	(Church, 1940)
TY_2	t, e, s	(Gallin, 1975)
TY_2 (alt.)	t, e, p [propositions]	(Thomason, 1980)
TY_3	t, e, s, d [degrees]	(Bylinina, 2013)
TY_3 (alt.)	t, e, s, p	(Muskens, 2005)
AHS (TY_3)	$t, e, p, \boldsymbol{i}$ [individual concepts]	(Pollard, 2008b, 2015)
TY_4	t, e, s, l [location], z [time]	(Liefke & Werning, 2018)
TY_5	t, e, v [events], i [intervals], d, n [numbers]	(Champollion, 2017)
TY_5 (alt.)	t, e, s, v, d, k [kinds]	(Rett, p.c.)
TY_7	t, s, v, l, z, σ [states], α [active entities], β [passive entities]	(Bittner, 2003)

(26) Matti is sleeping.

To mark the use of three truth-combinations, some theories superscript their type system's name with the number 3 (see, e.g., Muskens' 1995 system TY_2^3). The absence of a superscript is taken to reflect a restriction to the classical truth-values, **T** and **F** (i.e. as in ' TY_n^2'). I will return to the generalization of possible worlds to situations in Section 6.3.2.

6.3 Strategy 3: Generalize Basic Types

Interestingly, a proliferation of basic types can be limited by associating existing basic types with larger domains of objects, or by merging different semantic types. I will describe several such moves in what follows. These include the generalization of concrete individuals to abstract individuals (incl. kinds and degrees; see Section 6.3.1), the generalization of possible worlds to situations and events (see Section 6.3.2), and the generalization of situations to individuals (see Section 6.3.3).

It is often assumed that, although these generalizations help reduce the number of basic types, they only shift the proliferation of basic types to another level: the level or subtypes, or sorts. While this strategy indeed does not increase the theory's simplicity or parsimony (see my remarks at the beginning of Section 7), it straightforwardly explains why some proforms can be used for elements of intuitively distinct semantic categories (see my observations from Section 2.1.2). The treatment of different categories as subtypes within a single type also facilitates an account of cross-categorial entailments like (43), as I will show in Section 7.1.

6.3.1 Kinds, Degrees, and Content Individuals

Kinds. To capture linguistic support for kinds (see e.g. (18c)), Carlson (1977) and Chierchia (1998) have proposed to treat kinds k as a type-e subtype (see also McNally, 1992; McNally & Boleda, 2004; Zamparelli, 1995). Specifically, Chierchia's account treats kinds as individual correlates of properties that are obtained from properties through the nominalization operator *nom*, or $^{\cap}$ (read 'down'; see Chierchia, 1984; Chierchia & Turner, 1988).[21] This operator is a partial function that sends properties of individuals (type $\langle s, \langle e, t\rangle\rangle$) to individuals (type e). It can be introduced either by a kind-selecting predicate (and an associated shifting of the type of the DP to the subtype 'kind'; see Chierchia, 1998) or by a semantically loaded interpretation of the null determiner (i.e. as the function $P^{\langle s, \langle e,t\rangle\rangle} \mapsto {}^{\cap}P$; see Dayal, 2022). Both approaches (in (48a-i) and (48a-ii)) interpret (48a) as (48b), where **otterhound** is a predicate of the type $\langle s, \langle e, t\rangle\rangle$ and **rare** is a predicate of the type $\langle s, \langle k, t\rangle\rangle$.

(48) a. Otterhounds are rare.
   i. $[_{NP}$Otterhounds$]$ are rare.
   ii. $[_{DP}\emptyset\,[_{NP}$Otterhounds$]]$ are rare.
 b. **rare**(@, $^{\cap}$**otterhound**)

Note that, in contrast to what we have required, Montague's individual domain is restricted to concrete individuals. The latter are ordinary particulars (like Matti or my coffee mug) that are extended in space and time. To make the kind-interpretation of nouns like *Otterhound* in (48a) possible, Chierchia extends Montague's domain of individuals (his *urelements*, subtype u) to individual correlates of properties (i.e. the objects in the range of $^{\cap}$; Chierchia's *nominalized functions*, subtype nf). These correlates are abstract entities that may not be extended in space or time. Rather, they are *realized* – or *instantiated* – by objects that are located in space and time (Carlson, 1977; see McNally & Boleda, 2004; Zamparelli, 1995). The result of extending Montague's individual domain with nominalized functions is illustrated in Figure 10 (inspired by Chierchia & Turner, 1988, 266).

Degrees. A similar argument has been proposed for the adoption of type-e degrees (Cartwright, 1975; Klein, 1980; Parsons, 1970; see [5], [13]). Degrees represent quantities that are assigned by measure functions such as height,

[21] An extensional version of this operator is described in Partee (1987).

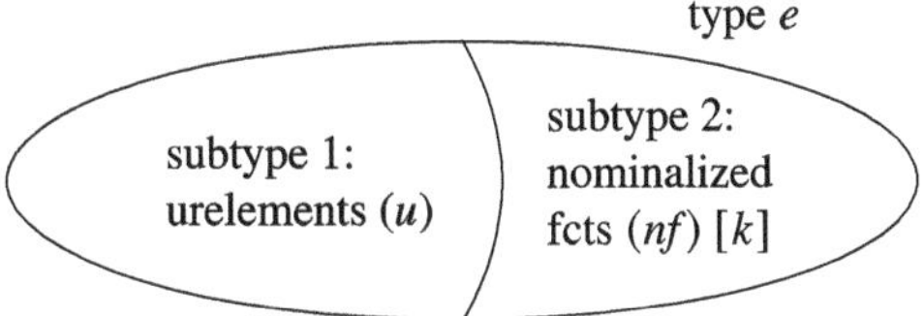

Figure 10 Partitioned individual domain, with urelements and kinds.

weight, or temperature (see Champollion, 2017, 29). Examples of degrees are Jane's height [= the degree to which Jane is tall] (1.68 m), Bill's height (1.89 m), and the temperature in my office on January 9, 2023, at 4:53 p.m. (i.e. 19.2° C).[22] This already suggests that degrees are totally ordered (thus forming a scale) and may – but need not – have a minimum/maximum.

The treatment of kinds and degrees as different subtypes of individuals straightforwardly explains both (i) the selectional differences between kind- and degree-denoting expressions (see (49)) and (ii) the fact that, in some languages (e.g. German), kinds and degrees share the same proforms (there: *so* ['such']; see (50); due to Umbach & Ebert, 2009). This explanation assumes that selection is determined at the level of subtype, while referential morphology is governed by the superordinate type-level.

(49) a. Javan rhinos
b. ??Jane's height/??the temperature in my office
} are rare/extinct.

(50) a. So einen Hund will ich auch! (kind)
Such a dog want I too.
'I want a dog of this/the same kind.'

b. Ich bin so groß. (degree)
I am such tall.
'I am this tall.'

Given the need to explain the shared degree- and kind-reference of *so* in (50) for German, the treatment of kinds and degrees as different subtypes (within the same basic type) is expected to be more fruitful than their treatment as distinct basic types.

Content individuals. To provide an adequate semantics for content DPs (e.g. the different arguments in (51)), Kratzer (2006) has proposed to extend Montague's type-*e* domain by content individuals (see also Moltmann, 2013, 2017, 2020). The latter are objects that carry propositional information content (in

[22] This Element was written in the midst of the German energy crisis.

(51a–c): the proposition '(that) Fred left'). They include abstract objects like fears, beliefs, and rumors as well as concrete particulars like the specific print exemplar of my favorite book. Since concrete particulars are already included in Montague's individual domain, concrete content-bearing particulars form a subset of Chierchia's *urelements*. Abstract content individuals require a genuine extension of the domain in Figure 10.

(51) a. the rumor
b. Mary's fear
c. Tom's belief } that Fred left

At first blush, one may be inclined to identify abstract content individuals with individual correlates of propositions (analyzed as zero-place versions of Chierchia's *nominalized functions*). However, the existence of a single proposition '(that) Fred left' and of multiple content individuals (in (51)) suggests that this cannot be right.

To identify the propositional content of the individuals that are denoted by the arguments in (51), Kratzer (2013) (following Kratzer, 2006) has proposed to introduce a content-related domain projection function, CONT.[23] This function identifies the propositional content of a content individual (see Elliott, 2017; Hacquard, 2006; Moulton, 2015). For example, for Mary's fear that Fred left (see (51b)), this function yields the proposition that Fred left – analyzed as the set of possible worlds in which Fred left (see (52)).

(52) CONT(Mary's fear that Fred left) = $\{w : \text{Fred left in } w\}$

Using the function CONT, we can specify a defining property, viz. contentfulness, of the type-e subtype 'content individual'.

Property 1 (contentfulness). An individual a is *contentful* (or 'carries propositional content') if there is a proposition, p, that the function CONT identifies as the content of a, that is, if $(\exists p)[\text{CONT}(a) = p]$.

Note that, since the subtype 'content individual' includes both abstract individuals (e.g. Mary's fear that Fred left) and concrete individuals (e.g. Mary's favorite book), it cuts across the subtypes u and nf. (This is why the separating line between content individuals and urelements resp. nominalized functions in Figure 11 is dashed.) Since type systems like the one in Figure 11 draw fine-grained ontological distinctions without assuming a large number of basic types (i.e. by subtyping), Rett (2022) calls their underlying strategy *type Ersatzism*.

[23] The name 'CONT' is due to Moulton (2015). Kratzer (2013) calls this function f_{content}.

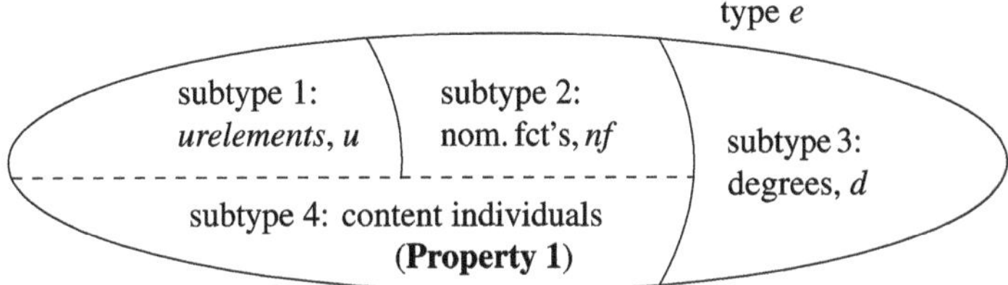

Figure 11 Partitioned individual domain with urelements, kinds, degrees, and content individuals.

6.3.2 Situations and Events

Situations. To accommodate situations in a TY_2 ontology, some theories have proposed to generalize the type for possible worlds, *s*, to partial possible worlds (i.e. to *situations*; Muskens, 1995; Schulz, 1993; see Section 6.1.2). Situations are spatio-temporal parts of possible worlds that are obtained by restricting a particular spatial location in a world to a particular time in the world's history (Kratzer, 2002; see also Liefke & Werning, 2018). This restriction is supported by the observation that "modal/temporal/spatial restrictions covary in a predictable way, [s.t.] a semantics that model[s] them independently can't be restrictive enough" (Rett, 2022, 290; based on Cresswell, 1990; Kratzer, 2019; Stone, 1997). This point is illustrated by the sentence in (53) (due to Kratzer, 2019):

(53) If, whenever it snowed, it had snowed much more than it actually did, the town plow would have removed the snow for us.

In particular, in (53), *would* cannot only range over possible snowing events. Rather, it must range over possible snowing events relativized to a particular location and (reference) time (Rett, 2022, 290).

To explicitly connect situations to worlds, many situation-semantic theories assume that situations are ordered by a spatial and a temporal inclusion relation, $\leq_l$ (for '<u>l</u>ocation') and $\leq_t$ (for '<u>t</u>ime'; see Liefke & Werning, 2018, 657–659; inspired by Muskens, 1995, chapter 7; anticipated by Barwise, 1989). The combination of these relations, $\leq$ (without a subscript), is Kratzer's (2002) partial ordering on situations. Different $\leq$-chains all share the same minimum, that is, the 'empty' situation, †.[24] Distinct chains differ with respect to their maximum (viz. different possible worlds; Kratzer, 2002). As a result, it holds for each situation σ that $\dagger \leq \sigma \leq w$, where w is some possible world.

[24] The assumption of a single minimal situation, †, – rather than of multiple such situations – is justified by the observation that the spatial and temporal dimensions of this situation are both empty, such that † is no longer part of a specific world.

The description of possible worlds as $\leq_l$- and $\leq_t$-maximal situations provides a property for the identification of the type-*s* subtype of worlds (see **Property 2**). In what follows '$\sigma <_l \sigma'$' is my shorthand for proper spatial inclusion (i.e. $\sigma <_l \sigma' := (\sigma \leq_l \sigma' \wedge \sigma \neq_l \sigma')$). I use an analogous shorthand, $<_t$, for proper temporal inclusion.

Property 2 (spatio-temporal maximality). A situation σ is a *spatio-temporally maximal element* of the type-*s* domain iff $\neg(\exists\sigma')[\sigma <_l \sigma' \vee \sigma <_t \sigma']$.

An advantage of separating $\leq_t$ from $\leq_l$ is that the temporal and the spatial dimensions of a possible world can be separately manipulated. As a result, theories that support this separation can identify both (spatially total) *time-slices* of worlds (i.e. the world at a given point in time) and *total histories* of a certain location in a world. The latter are the $\leq_l$-maximal and the $\leq_t$-maximal situations.

Note that a generalization of W along these lines in fact involves *two* (!) extensions of W: The first of these is the extension of W by additional, 'smaller' worlds/situations (yielding a set of larger cardinality and greater ontological diversity). The second extension lies in the introduction of a (multidimensional) algebraic structure on this set (induced by $\leq_l$ and $\leq_t$). However, since these extensions are independently supported – and since they are also required by other approaches (see, e.g., Moltmann, 1995) – they do not compromise the parsimony of situation subtyping.

Events. The joint availability of $\leq_l$ and $\leq_t$ also enables a situation-semantic account of Davidsonian events (Davidson, 2001; see my discussion of (16)–(17)). The latter are spatially and temporally bounded constituents of worlds that have a single occurrence (Champollion, 2017, 27; see Carlson, 1998), that have proper (temporal) parts, and that can themselves be parts of larger events (see Bach, 1986b; Krifka, 1998). This characterization straightforwardly identifies events as a subtype of situation.

Importantly, though, in contrast to 'vanilla' situations, events have a built-in minimality condition (Kratzer, 2019, section 9). Minimality is required to capture the intuitive truth-conditions of event-sentences like (54): (54) is only true in scenarios in which there was singing by John that took a full hour. It is intuitively false in scenarios in which John sang for five minutes and filled the remaining time of the reported hour by drinking coffee, reading the newspaper, and clipping his nails (see Kratzer, 2019).

(54) John's singing lasted an hour.

To capture the informational minimality of the event reported in (54), Kratzer (2019) identifies this event with a situation that *exemplifies* the proposition 'John is singing.' The latter is a situation that only makes this proposition true, and that does not make any other proposition (e.g. 'John is drinking coffee', . . ., 'Mary is sorting her references') true (see Kratzer, 2002). In virtue of this, events are a subtype of situation whose elements have the property of minimal exemplification (see **Property 3**). This property amounts to the absence of proper parts in which the proposition is false (or undefined):

Property 3 (minimal exemplification). A situation σ *minimally exemplifies* a proposition p iff $p(\sigma) \wedge \neg(\exists\sigma')[\sigma' < \sigma \wedge \neg p(\sigma')]$.

Obviously, to support (54)'s truth in a scenario in which John's singing took a whole hour, the referenced 'John singing' -event needs to be extended in time: A temporally minimal event in which John is only singing for a very short period of time would make (54) false (see Kratzer, 2019). Since minimal exemplification of the proposition 'John is singing the song' is only possible for situations that are inhabited by John – and since John himself takes up a(n admittedly small) region of space – minimally exemplifying situations must also be extended in space. The spatial and temporal dimensions of situations straightforwardly provide the thematic roles '**loc**' and '**time**' (see (17)). The comparatively small size of events reduces the number of concrete individuals that could serve as the semantic values of referential DPs to a manageable set. The lexical entry for the matrix verb (above: *sing*) provides the thematic roles that identify different members of this set (see Kratzer, 1996; Landman, 1996).

Accomplishments and achievements. The temporal ordering on situations, $\leq_t$, also enables a distinction between Vendlerian (1957) *accomplishments* and *achievements*. Accomplishments and achievements are subtypes of events that differ with respect to their temporal extendedness: While accomplishments (e.g. drawing a circle, writing a book) have a temporal extension, achievements (e.g. reaching the summit, recognizing Peter) are instantaneous events (i.e. momentary changes of state that have no temporal duration; see Maienborn, 2011, 810). To answer the challenge that such events pose to mainstream event semantics (see, e.g., Krifka, 1989; Parsons, 1990), Piñón (1997, 291) defines achievements as "happenings that both end a happening [e.g. finishing one's climb] and begin a state [e.g. being at the summit]." The existence of instantaneous and temporally extended events straighforwardly explains the selectional differences between accomplishments and achievements (see (55), (56); inspired by Vendler, 1957):

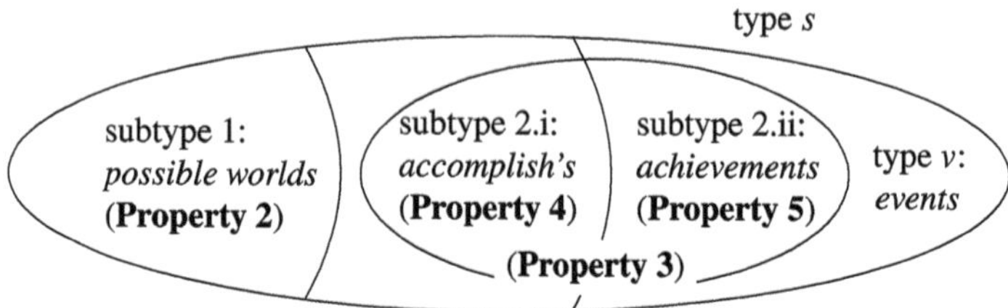

Figure 12 Partitioned situation domain with subtypes for situations, events, accomplishments, and achievements.

(55) a. John wrote the book } for three years/until he was 40.
b. ??John reached the top

(56) a. ??John wrote the book } at 10:53 a.m./at noon sharp.
b. John reached the top

Sorting events with respect to their temporal (non-)extendedness (see **Properties 4** and **5**) straightforwardly accounts for this behavior.

Property 4 (temporal extendedness). A situation σ is *temporally extended* if it has a proper temporal part, that is, $(\exists\sigma')[\sigma' <_t \sigma]$.

Property 5 (temporal non-extendedness). A situation σ is <u>not</u> *temporally extended* if it does *not* have a proper temporal part, that is, $\neg(\exists\sigma')[\sigma' <_t \sigma]$.

The partitioning of the type-s domain that results from applying **Properties 2** to **5** is sketched in Figure 12.

6.3.3 Merge Individuals and Events

My previous discussion has described situations as very versatile entities that unify different subtypes. The versatility of situations may be taken to suggest that individuals can also be conceived of as situations. This view has been defended in some work on situation semantics (esp. Kratzer, 1989, 613–614). Following Armstrong (1980) and Lewis (1986), Kratzer (1989) distinguishes between 'thin' and 'thick' particulars. This distinction assumes that, for each property, P, of an individual x, x's having P defines an x-situation, or *state of affairs* (i.e. the situation that minimally exemplifies '$P(x)$'; cf. Bianchi, 2017, 10). A thin individual is then the $\leq$-based 'meet' of all x-situations (intuitively, the situation that minimally exemplifies 'x exists'). A thick individual is the $\leq$-based 'join' of all such situations (intuitively, the situation that minimally exemplifies the conjunction '$P_{(0)}(x) \wedge P_1(x) \wedge \ldots P_n(x)$', where $P_0 \ldots P_n$ are exactly all of x's properties). The latter is a larger situation of which it, however, holds that none of its proper parts does *not* contain x.

Bianchi (2017) has pointed out that the availability of thin and thick particulars corresponds to the interpretation of referential DPs between individuals and generalized quantifiers (see Bianchi, 2017, fn. 10). For simplicity, I assume that individuals (i.e. elements of Montague's domain A) are represented by thin particulars. Being a thin particular (see **Property 6**) then defines the type-s subtype 'individual':

Property 6 (being a thin particular). A situation σ is a *thin particular* if it minimally exemplifies the proposition 'x exists' for some individual x.

Note that the subtype of thin particulars cuts across the boundary of the subtype of events. This due to the fact that, like the subtype 'event', the subtype 'thin particular' is defined with reference to the property of minimal exemplification. As a result, the situation-denoting term in (57) will represent both John and the event – or state – of John's existing. In (57), '$E(\sigma, \mathbf{john})$' asserts that John *inhabits* (or *exists in*) the situation σ.

(57) $\iota\sigma.\, E(\sigma, \mathbf{john}) \wedge \neg(\exists\sigma')[\sigma' < \sigma \wedge \neg E(\sigma', \mathbf{john})]$

This completes my review of attempts to represent intuitively different semantic entities in the same basic type. Arguably, as is apparent from Figures 10 to 12, merging types will not automatically result in a more parsimonious ontology: The number of sorts that are introduced through this procedure in fact *matches* the number of 'original' basic types. Since many of these sorts are obtained by properly extending Montague's original domains (e.g. to abstract and/or to partial entities) and by introducing an algebraic structure on the resulting domain (e.g. through the relations $\leq_l$ and $\leq_t$), it could even be argued that these attempts add complexity. Section 7 discusses recent efforts to avoid this problem.

7 Type Unification and Meta-Ontology

In the past few years, some researchers have proposed to obtain genuinely more parsimonious ontologies by unifying semantic categories. Section 7.1 identifies two recent efforts in this direction, that is, inquisitive semantics (Ciardelli, Groenendijk, & Roelofsen, 2013; Ciardelli et al., 2018) and single-type semantics[25] (Liefke, 2014; Liefke & Werning, 2018; following Partee, 2009). From

[25] Sutton (2024) calls single-type semantics 'monotype(d) semantics'.

these efforts, Section 7.2 draws some lessons about the trade-off between simplicity and parsimony, about the relation between the ontological object- and metatheory, and about the engineering of semantic ontologies more generally.

7.1 Unification

A key ingredient to providing an ontologically modest unifying type lies in identifying this type with a *complex Boolean* type.[26] In contrast to the basic-type domains from Section 6.3, Boolean domains are naturally endowed with an algebraic structure (induced by set-theoretic inclusion) and often allow the definition of further structures (see e.g. Muskens, 1995; Roelofsen, 2013). As a result, they obviate the introduction of 'new' ordering relations. Unlike basic-type domains, the elements in complex-type domains are typically not all needed as semantic values (note that Partee's [1987] type-shifter, LIFT, which maps individuals to generalized quantifiers, is only injective [*one-to-one*], but not surjective [*onto*]). As a result, complex-type domains already include the 'extra objects' whose basic-type correlates the theories from Section 6.3 add to Montague's original domain(s).

Next, I show how inquisitive semantics and single-type semantics succeed in unifying types. These semantic theories share the restriction to TY_2 types (although single-type semantics associates the type s with situations).[27] They also share the same general strategy for obtaining unified types (viz. type-shifting). To a large extent, the two theories even have the same empirical motivation (to be discussed in Section 7.1.2). They differ with respect to their intended domain of unification (propositions and questions vis-à-vis propositions and individuals) and to their specific meta-ontological consequences (see Section 7.2).

7.1.1 Unifying Propositions and Questions

To capture the selectional flexibility of responsive predicates like *know* and *report* (exemplified in (58) and (59); see also (12c/d)), Theiler et al. (2018) have proposed to interpret both declaratives and interrogatives in the semantic type for questions, $\langle\langle s,t\rangle,t\rangle$ (see also Ciardelli, Roelofsen, & Theiler, 2017). This interpretation waives the familiar distinction between propositions and questions in favor of a single type of semantic value.

---

26 For a detailed presentation of this argument, the reader is referred to Liefke (2014, chapter 4).

27 To avoid generalizing TY_2 types along these lines, one could represent situations σ by the set of all possible worlds that are maximal extensions of σ, $\{w : w \geq \sigma\}$. Possible worlds would then be represented by singleton sets. However, since this representation further complicates the 'basic' single-type type, I refrain from using this representation.

(58) Mia knows/reports $\left\{\begin{array}{l}\text{a. } \textbf{that} \text{ John was singing} \\ \text{b. } \textbf{who} \text{ was singing/}\textbf{whether} \text{ John was singing}\end{array}\right\}$.

(59) Mia knows [**that** John was singing a song] and [**who** taught it to him].

To obtain a question-interpretation for declaratives, Theiler et al. lift propositions to questions through the type-shifter $p^{\langle s,t\rangle} \mapsto \{q : q \subseteq p\}$. This shifter sends sets of worlds p to their powersets, $\mathcal{P}(p)$, that is, to downward-closed sets of propositions (see Section 6.1.1; Figure 9b). They assume that this type-shifter is already built into the lexical semantics of all non-referential expressions. These expressions are assigned a type that 'ends in $\langle\langle s,t\rangle,t\rangle$', rather than in $\langle s,t\rangle$ (see Section 5: Table 7). The uniform-type values for the constituents of the *that*-clause in (58a) are given in (60) (based on Ciardelli et al., 2017). For better availability, I have added types in superscript in (60).

(60) a. John $\rightsquigarrow$ $\mathbf{john}^e$

b. sing $\rightsquigarrow$ $\lambda x^e \lambda q^{\langle s,t\rangle}.\, q \subseteq \{w : \mathbf{sing}(w,x)\}$
$\equiv \lambda x.\, \mathcal{P}(\{w : \mathbf{sing}(w,x)\})$

c. that $\rightsquigarrow$ $\lambda T^{\langle\langle s,t\rangle,t\rangle} \lambda p.\, T(p)$

(61) that John sings $\rightsquigarrow$ $\lambda T \lambda p.\, T(p)\ ((\lambda x.\, \mathcal{P}(\{w : \mathbf{sing}(w,x)\}))(\mathbf{john}))$
$\equiv \lambda p.\, p \subseteq \{w : \mathbf{sing}(w, \mathbf{john})\}$
$\equiv \mathcal{P}(\{w : \mathbf{sing}(w, \mathbf{john})\})$

Notably, the specification of the semantic value of *sing* in (60b) still uses the non-logical type-$\langle e, \langle s,t\rangle\rangle$ constant '**sing**' (which denotes a function from individuals to propositions). I will return to this observation in Section 7.2.

The interpretations in (60)–(61) assume a single, uniform domain for the semantic values of sentences. For declaratives and interrogatives, these values are downwards-closed sets of propositions (i.e. Ciardelli et al.'s *inquisitive meanings*). While some of these values (e.g. (61), (62b)) likely serve as interpretations of declaratives and, respectively, of interrogatives, others are expectedly ambiguous between declaratives and interrogatives. This holds for inquisitive meanings that have multiple maximal elements. One such meaning (in (63c)) provides the interpretation of the declarative in (63a) and the interrogative in (63b).

(62) a. who $\rightsquigarrow$ $\lambda \mathfrak{P}^{\langle e,\langle\langle s,t\rangle,t\rangle\rangle}.\, \bigcup_{x\in A} \mathfrak{P}(x)$

b. who sings? $\rightsquigarrow$ $\bigcup_{x\in A} \mathcal{P}(\{w : \mathbf{sing}(w,x)\})$

(63) a. John sings or Mary dances.

b. Does John sing or Mary dance?

c. $\rightsquigarrow$ $\mathcal{P}(\{w : \mathbf{sing}(w, \mathbf{John}) \vee \mathbf{dance}(w, \mathbf{Mary})\})$

Note that, in contrast to Pollard's hyperintensional semantics (which uses some of the 'ingredient' types for world-representations, that is, primitive propositions, as semantic values for other expressions; see Section 6.1.2), inquisitive semantics does not use propositions as an independent semantic category. In fact, much work in inquisitive semantics replaces the type label '$\langle\langle s,t\rangle,t\rangle$' by '$T$' (see e.g. Ciardelli et al., 2017; Theiler et al., 2018). Consequently, we can treat $\langle\langle s,t\rangle,t\rangle$ as a non-decomposable type. By replacing the type for propositions by the type for questions (which, one may argue, are needed anyway), inquisitive semantics thus *reduces* the semantic ontology by one category!

Importantly, inquisitive semantics owes its greater parsimony to the fact that it uniformly interprets all clausal complements in the same type, that is, as questions (see (60c), (61)). Theories that only lift propositions to questions 'on demand' – and, hence, still use propositions as the default semantic values of declaratives (see e.g. Uegaki, 2016, 2019) – do not share this parsimony.

7.1.2 Merits of Complex-Type Unification

I have suggested that a uniform interpretation of declaratives and interrogatives helps capture the selectional flexibility of responsive predicates (see (12c/d), (58)) and the availability of coordinations that connect declarative and interrogative clauses (see (59)). Importantly, this interpretation is still compatible both with the traditional assumption that predicates select for a single type of argument (thus capturing selectional restrictions like the ones in Section 2.1.1; see (64)/(69a)) and with the assumption that coordination is restricted to expressions of the same semantic type (thus excluding certain instances of declarative/interrogative coordination, like [65]).

(64) Eve believes {**that**, ??**whether**, ??**which** song} John was singing.

(65) ??Eve believes [**that** John was singing the song] and [**who** taught it to him].

Semantic inclusion. Expectedly, the same-type (and same-sort) interpretation of declaratives and interrogatives in inquisitive semantics also captures their intuitive semantic inclusion relations. These relations are evidenced by the valid entailment from (66a) to (66b) and by the equivalence of (67a) and (67b). They also account for the redundancy of reports like (67a) (see Liefke, 2021).

(66) a. Mia knows [**that** John is singing].

⇒ b. Mia knows [**whether** John is singing].

(67) a. #Mia knows [**whether** John is singing (a song)] and [**that** he is singing the Marseillaise].

≡ b. Mia knows [**that** John is singing the Marseillaise].

On an intuitive level, the validity of entailments like (66) is ascribed to the observation that the information of the embedded interrogative in (66b) (i.e. 'John is or is not singing') is contained in the information of the embedded declarative in (66a) (i.e. 'John is singing'). The redundancy – and attendant markedness – of the conjunction (67a) is due to the fact that the true answer to the question that is denoted by the first conjunct in the complement of (67a) (viz. 'John is singing a song') is informationally contained in the content of the second conjunct in (67a) (viz. 'John is singing the Marseillaise'). The uniform interpretation of declaratives and interrogatives as downward-closed sets of propositions straightforwardly accounts for this relation; see (68):[28]

(68) a. that John is singing the Marseillaise
$\rightsquigarrow \lambda p\left[p \subseteq \{w : \mathbf{sing}(w, \mathbf{john}, \mathbf{marseillaise})\}\right]$

⇒ b. whether John is singing (a song)
$\rightsquigarrow \lambda p\,(\exists x)\big[p \subseteq \{w : \mathbf{sing}(w, \mathbf{john}, x)\} \vee (\forall q \subseteq \{w : \mathbf{sing}(w, \mathbf{john})\} : p \cap q = \emptyset)\big]$

Selection. The same-type interpretation of declaratives and interrogatives also provides a semantic account of selectional restrictions (see, e.g., Theiler et al., 2019; Uegaki & Sudo, 2019). Such an account is required by the observation that, in inquisitive semantics, the selection behavior of clause-embedding predicates can no longer be explained through differences in semantic type (see Section 3.2). It is made possible by the observation that predicates with similar semantic properties display a similar selection behavior (but see the caveats in White, 2021). This observation includes the systematic correlation between anti-rogativity and neg-raising[29] (Mayr, 2019; Theiler et al., 2019; Zuber, 1982; see (69a)) and between anti-rogativity and the combination of preferentiality with non-veridicality (Uegaki & Sudo, 2019; see (69b)). Instances of these correlations are given below:

(69) a. Eve thinks/believes/expects {**that**, ??**whether**, ??**which** song} John sang.

b. Eve wishes/hopes/fears {**that**, ??**whether**, ??**which** song} John sang.

---

[28] This interpretation assumes a simple, type-adjusted semantics for *whether*, according to which 'whether' $\rightsquigarrow \lambda T \lambda p[T(p) \vee \neg\!\!\neg\, T(p)]$. In the specification of this semantics, $\neg\!\!\neg := \{p : (\forall q \in T : p \wedge q = \emptyset)\}$ is inquisitive negation (see Theiler, Roelofsen, & Aloni, 2019).

[29] Neg-raising predicates are predicates V that license the inference from 'NP not-V S' to 'NP V not-S'. This form of inference is exemplified in (70a) ⇒ (70c).

To account for these correlations, Theiler et al. (2019) assume that neg-raising predicates like *think* and *believe* semantically involve an excluded middle (EM)-presupposition. For the occurrence of *believe* in (70a), this presupposition (in (70b)) assumes that Eve is opinionated as to whether John sang (Theiler et al., 2019, 102).

(70) a. Eve does **not** believe that John sang.
b. *Presupposition:* 'Either Eve believes that John sang or Eve believes that John did **not** sing'
⇒ c. Eve believes that John did **not** sing.

While the EM-presupposition yields the desired neg-raising effect for reports with declarative complements (see (70)), its contribution is already asserted by reports in which a neg-raising predicate combines with a polar interrogative complement. In these reports, the asserted content of the complement is trivial relative to the presupposition of the relevant occurrence of *believe* (Theiler et al., 2019, 106):

(71) a. *Eve believes whether John sang.
[≡ Eve believes: John sang or John did **not** sing]
b. *Presupposition:* 'Either Eve believes that John sang or Eve believes that John did **not** sing'
⇒ c. ⊤ (trivial)

Since this triviality is systematic (i.e. independent of the sentence's specific lexical material), it is perceived as a grammatical unacceptability (Gajewski, 2007; Theiler et al., 2019). This explains the anti-rogativity of *believe.*

Uegaki and Sudo (2019) have presented a similar account of the anti-rogativity of predicates like *hope* and *fear*. Much current work on clausal embedding is concerned with extending this approach to further classes of predicates (incl. emotive factives and veridical and counterfactual representational predicates, e.g. *remember*, *imagine*; see Liefke, 2023a; Ózyildiz, Qing, Roelofsen, et al., 2022). Type-uniform accounts of selectional restrictions thus promise to make an important contribution to carving natural language ontology 'at its joints'.

7.1.3 Unifying Individuals and Propositions

My discussion up to now has focused on attempts to unify the semantic counter-parts of related syntactic categories (in Sections 7.1.1–7.1.2: different sentence types). While these attempts diverge from traditional assumptions about semantic ontological categories (see Sections 3–6), they do not question Montague's core ontological distinction, that is, the separation of individuals (type e) from propositions (type $\langle s, t\rangle$). In a short paper entitled "Do We Need Two Basic Types?", Partee (2009) challenges this distinction. In particular, she conjectures that the key merits of Montague-style formal semantics (i.e. explaining acceptability, truth, and entailment) can be preserved in a semantics that merges e and $\langle s, t\rangle$ (or p) into a single basic type.

Liefke and Werning (2018) (based on Liefke, 2014) provide further support for Partee's conjecture. This support takes a very similar form to the support for Theiler et al.'s uniform interpretation of declaratives and interrogatives. It includes:

- a predicate's selectional flexibility between CPs and referential DPs (see (12a/ c) and (72), compare (58); Kim, 2008; Lohndal, 2017)
- the possibility of coordinating CPs with referential DPs (see (73), compare (59); Bayer, 1996; Sag, Wasow, & Bender, 1999)
- the existence of semantic inclusion relations between CPs and referential DPs (see (74), compare (66)–(67))

The same-type interpretation of CPs and referential DPs is moreover supported by propositional anaphora (see (15c) and (75); Asher, 1993; Potts, 2002). The examples below are taken from Liefke and Werning (2018). In (74b), '$\overset{c}{\equiv}$' marks contextual equivalence.

(72)

Pat noticed/remembered/imagined { a. Bill. / b. **that** Bill was waiting for her. }

(73) Pat remembered [Bill] and [**that** he was waiting for her].

(74) *Context:* Barbara Partee is arriving at a linguistics conference. A participant turns to her colleague, gestures towards Partee, and utters (a):

a. The keynote speaker.

$\overset{c}{\equiv}$ b. The keynote speaker is arriving.

(75) Mary believes [**that** Bill has feelings for Pat]$_i$. John is certain of it$_i$.

To account for phenomena like (72)–(75), Liefke and Werning (2018) have proposed to drop Montague's types e and $\langle s, t\rangle$ in favor of the single complex type

$\langle s, \langle s, t \rangle \rangle$.[30] The latter is the type for functions from informationally poor 'initializing situations' σ_0 to sets of situations $\{\sigma : \sigma_0 \leq \sigma\}$ (where '$\leq$' is the partial ordering on situations from Section 6.3.2). Liefke and Werning treat $\langle s, \langle s, t \rangle \rangle$ as a non-decomposable – and hence, basic – type, and abbreviate '$\langle s, \langle s, t \rangle \rangle$' as '$o$' (analogously to Theiler et al.'s 'T'). In line with a Montague-style type hierarchy, they still assume function spaces over o (using **Rule 1**). The resulting set of types includes, e.g., the type $\langle o, o \rangle$ (for sentential negation, common nouns, and intransitive verbs) and $\langle o, \langle o, o \rangle \rangle$ (for sentential conjunction and transitive verbs).

In Liefke and Werning's single-type semantics, referential DPs like *Bill* or *the keynote speaker* from (72a)/(74a) are then interpreted as (76a/b). Declarative sentences like *Bill waits for Pat* receive an interpretation of the form of (77). In (76) to (78), E is a situation-relative existence predicate. '$E(\sigma,x)$' asserts that the individual x exists in (or 'inhabits') the situation σ.

(76) a. Bill $\rightsquigarrow \lambda\sigma_0.\, \{\sigma : \sigma_0 \leq \sigma \wedge E(\sigma, \mathbf{bill})\}$

b. the keynote speaker

$\rightsquigarrow \lambda\sigma_0(\iota x).\, \{\sigma : \sigma_0 \leq \sigma \wedge (\mathbf{keynote\text{-}speaker}(\sigma,x) \wedge E(\sigma,x))\}$

$\equiv \lambda\sigma_0(\iota x).\, \{\sigma : \sigma_0 \leq \sigma \wedge \mathbf{keynote\text{-}speaker}(\sigma,x)\}$

(77) Bill waits for Pat.

$\rightsquigarrow \lambda\sigma_0.\, \{\sigma : \sigma_0 \leq \sigma \wedge (E(\sigma, \mathbf{bill}) \wedge \mathbf{wait\text{-}for}(\sigma, \mathbf{bill}, \mathbf{pat}))\}$

$\equiv \lambda\sigma_0.\, \{\sigma : \sigma_0 \leq \sigma \wedge \mathbf{wait\text{-}for}(\sigma, \mathbf{bill}, \mathbf{pat})\}$

(76a) identifies the single-type semantic value of *Bill* with a function from σ_0 to the set of extensions of σ_0 that are inhabited by Bill (see Liefke & Werning, 2018 for details). By definition, this extension may add information that is neither already included in σ_0 nor in the formula '$E(\sigma, \mathbf{bill})$'. The interpretations in (76) and (77) then straightforwardly explain the relation between CPs and referential DPs from (72) to (75).

Like inquisitive meanings (see (63)), basic single-type objects can even be ambiguous between the semantic value of a CP and a referential DP. The latter is the case in (78):

(78) Bill $\rightsquigarrow \lambda\sigma_0.\, \{\sigma : \sigma_0 \leq \sigma \wedge E(\sigma, \mathbf{bill})\}$ (see (76a))

$\leftsquigarrow$ (that) Bill exists

(78) shows that the semantic values of CPs and referential DPs in single-type semantics – like the values of declaratives and interrogatives in inquisitive semantics – do not correspond to sorts/subtypes. The absence of a semantic

30 For a detailed presentation of the reasons for this type choice, the reader is referred to Liefke (2014, Chapters 4–5).

distinction between CPs and referential DPs suggests that single-type semantics affords an analogous account of selectional restrictions to inquisitive semantics.[31]

Note that, since single-type semantics replaces the types e and $\langle s,t\rangle$ with a new type, $\langle s,\langle s,t\rangle\rangle$, it is prima facie not more parsimonious than inquisitive semantics. (This holds at least so long as one disregards the difference between unifying basic types and unifying a basic type with a complex type that is constructed from this type.) However, my previous considerations suggest a strategy for obtaining an even more parsimonious ontology. This strategy lies is identifying a higher-rank type (e.g. the type of Liefke's [2021] *parametrized centered questions*: $\langle s,\langle\langle s,t\rangle,t\rangle\rangle$) that codes both questions and basic single-type objects.

A brief glance at this common type for questions and single-type objects already shows that unifying semantic types comes at a (perhaps substantial) cost, that is, an increase of type complexity and a disconnect of the type system of the semantic metatheory from the type system of the semantic object theory. The penultimate subsection of this Element discusses this cost and attendant lessons for the engineering of semantic ontologies.

7.2 Semantic Types in Object- and Metatheory

7.2.1 Ontological Object- and Metalanguage

I have already pointed out that the specification of uniform-type objects (e.g. inquisitive meanings, basic single-type objects) still uses variables and constants for these objects' 'ingredient' types. In my description of the inquisitive meaning of *(that) John sings* (see (61)), these are the individual variable x, the world variable w, and the nonlogical type-$\langle e,\langle s,t\rangle\rangle$ constant **sing**. Similar observations hold for the description of the single-type values of *the keynote speaker* and *(that) Bill waits for Pat* (in (76b) and (77)). Admittedly, inquisitive semantics still assumes the basic types e and s. It uses these types in the type of common nouns and intransitive verbs, $\langle e,T\rangle$ (see (60b)), respectively in the type for intensions of declaratives or interrogatives, $\langle s,T\rangle$. However, if inquisitive meanings are treated as a non-decomposable type, it seems at least questionable to define them through the use of lower-type terms or objects (more on this below).

On top of this, the presence of internal structure (evidenced by simpler-type expressions like x and **sing**, and by the assumption of algebraic structure) is

[31] While a detailed such account is still forthcoming, I expect that this account will make an important contribution to the semantic ontology of natural language(s).

not merely an option for unifying objects – it is one of their key features: if these objects were unstructured entities (similar to Pollard's primitive propositions), the only way to account for semantic inclusion relations like (66)–(67) or (78) would be by stipulation. However, apart from failing to capture the context-dependency of some such relations (see e.g. (74)), this stipulation would seriously compromise compositionality and learnability.

To reconcile non-decomposability with the presence of internal structure, Liefke (2014) has proposed to distinguish the object theory of single-type semantics (which only assumes a single basic type, viz. $\langle s, \langle s, t\rangle\rangle$) from this semantics' metatheory (which is a partial version of TY_2, i.e. TY_2^3, with basic types for individuals, situations, and (partial) truth-combinations). Admittedly, dissociating the type systems of the object- and metatheory complicates the resulting semantic theory. However, the careful distinction between these type systems gives useful insights into the inner workings of our semantics' ontologies: Even if a single-type semantics (as envisioned by Partee, 2009) is, in principle, possible – at least at the level of the object theory – it still requires a multi-typed metatheory. Similar considerations may be used to disentangle the difficult semantic-ontological issues connected to Prior's puzzle (see e.g. Güngör, 2022; Moltmann, 2003, 2013; Prior, 1963, 1971).

7.2.2 The Simplicity/Parsimony Trade-Off

The distinction between object- and metatheory suggests a trade-off between parsimony and simplicity. For the present purposes, I understand parsimony as the existence of a low number of basic types and type-forming rules that are used to obtain the types (and associated semantic values) of linguistic expressions (see Section 3.3). Simplicity is the absence – or low complexity – of internal structure in the objects that serve as semantic values of these expressions.

As inquisitive and single-type semantics richly show, an increase in parsimony often goes along with the addition of internal structure (and an attendant decrease of simplicity). Inversely, an increase in simplicity (e.g. as exemplified by the restriction to unstructured – or, at most, partially ordered – objects) typically requires giving up some of the theory's ontological parsimony: without typal/sortal distinctions and internal structure, a semantics is neither able to account for the compositional computation of complex semantic values nor can it make correct predictions about truth and entailment (see Sections 6.3, 7.2.1).

My discussion from the previous three sections suggests that type-theoretic semantics (which identifies the semantic values of some expressions with objects of a complex type) achieves a pretty good balance between simplicity and parsimony: Adopting only basic types – or a very large number of such types – will lose the semantics' parsimony. Inversely, assuming only a single basic type that serves as the semantic value of all referential or clausal expressions (as in single-type semantics) will lose the semantics' simplicity. Needless to say, the 'perfect' ontology for the semantics of a natural language would be one that scores very high on the measures of both simplicity and parsimony (not to mention adequacy, together with various other desiderata; see Liefke, 2024b, section 1). However, I am afraid that – if such ontology should exist at all (of which I am doubtful) – we are still a long way from finding or engineering it.

8 Conclusion

This Element has discussed the foundational semantic ontology of natural language(s). It has identified this ontology with the result of identifying the basic building blocks in these languages' descriptive semantic commitments. The introductory sections (Sections 1–2) have reviewed the observation that – their dependence on the adopted semantic theory notwithstanding – the descriptive semantic ontologies of different languages show a substantial overlap. I have illustrated this overlap through the example of German and the Austronesian language Motu, whose descriptive ontologies share a commitment to, e.g., individuals, properties, propositions, events, and times – but not to degrees.

Sections 3 to 7 have shown that the observed overlap is significantly decreased when one moves from descriptive to foundational semantic ontologies. They have attributed this decrease to the possibility of obtaining the same descriptive ontology from different collections of basic categories (i.e. from different foundational/type-theoretic ontologies) and to the fact that the selection of basic categories is strongly influenced by the theory's objectives and external commitments (e.g. to abstract objects like content individuals and primitive propositions). Section 5 has identified the Frege-Church and the Russellian intensional ontology as extreme case of this variation. It has shown that, given plausible background assumptions, these ontologies do not share a single basic category. In particular, whereas the Russellian ontology interprets referential DPs and declarative sentences as individuals and, respectively, as primitive propositions, the Frege–Church ontology interprets these expressions as intensional generalized quantifiers and as sets of possible worlds.

While ontological differences of this kind are a natural part of theory pluralism, they pose a serious challenge to the project of providing a semantics for a representative, larger-size fragment of some natural language: When semantics for different phenomena make different assumptions about the semantic categories of their shared expressions, their results cannot be straightforwardly integrated. Thus, we can only combine a hyperintensional semantics for attitude predicates (which interprets embedded declaratives as primitive propositions; see Section 6.2.2) with a Kripke-style semantics for modals (see [18a], [24]) once we have established the relation between propositions and sets of worlds. Analogous considerations hold, for example, for the combination of attitude semantics with event semantics, and for the combination of event semantics with semantics for manner adverbs (which assume primitive manners) and with semantics for measure phrases (which assume degrees).

Some newer work has started to identify 'inter-ontology' (or inter-model) relations of this sort (see also Liefke, 2024b, section 5). For example, this work involves supplementing the intensional ontology of TY_2 with primitive propositions, and subsequently dropping primitive worlds (or indices) in favor of ultrafilters on propositions (see Section 6.1.2). A related example lies in the enrichment of Davidson's event-semantic ontology with manners, analyzed in terms of events and their properties (see Section 6.1.3). Following Thomason's (1980) top-down view of the intensional hierarchy (see Section 3.4),[32] some of this work has identified reduction relations between hyperintensional objects (e.g. primitive propositions), their intensional correlates (here: sets of possible worlds, or of situations), and these correlates' extensions (i.e. truth-values; see Muskens, 2005; Pollard, 2015). I am convinced that translational work of this kind is crucial for understanding the core requirements on a language's ontology: Much more of this work is needed to get the best out of our existing semantic theories.

Arguably, insights into the relations between different semantic ontologies still do not provide the ultimate ontology for a given language or fragment. I have shown in (Liefke, 2017) that semantic theories ontologically cluster in the sense that the ontologies of different semantic theories are equivalent with respect to their empirical adequacy and predictive power. (This holds e.g. for the intensional ontologies of IL, TY_2, and situation semantics; see also Zimmermann, 1989 and Muskens, 1995.) Which ontology in such a cluster a semantic theory ends up using depends (i) on this semantics' particular research agenda ['Does it pursue a descriptive, explanatory, or foundational project?'], (ii) on its particular weighting of criteria for theory (or model) choice ['Does the project care more about fruitfulness, simplicity, or parsimony?'],

[32] This view assumes a many-to-one relation between hyperintensions and intensions, and a many-to-one relation between intensions and extensions (Thomason, 1980; see Muskens, 2005).

and – unsurprisingly – (iii) on contemporary scientific and theoretical trends and standards ['Which ontological assumptions are made in related work?']. In the latter sense, a semantics' ontology will always be a child of its time.

All of this notwithstanding, recent work on selectional flexibility and semantic unification (see Section 7.1) may have opened a window to less biased ontologies. By design, this work strongly weights parsimony above simplicity (see Section 7.2). However, this uneven weighting is compensated by a careful distinction between the semantic ontology of the object- and the metatheory: In contrast to the ontology of the object theory, the ontology of the metatheory weights simplicity over parsimony. This is apparent from the metatheory of single-type semantics, which still assumes individuals (type *e*), possible situations (type *s*), truth-combinations (type *t*), and – arguably – events (type *v*). Given this observation, one could provide the following speculative alternative to Ritchie's (2016) criterion for being a category in *the* semantic ontology of a given natural language:

(Tentative) Criterion for being a category in a language's semantic ontology. A language carries a commitment to a certain ontological category *O* (i) if *O* is assumed in the metatheory of all competing (formal) semantic theories for this language *and* (ii) if *O* is assumed in the object theory of the simplest semantics for this language.

Since the metatheories of Montague's (IL/TY_2-based), inquisitive, and single-type semantics all assume individuals, the aforementioned criterion identifies individuals as a semantic category in the ontology of (contemporary extensions of) Montague's PTQ-fragment. This holds although Montague (1973) does not interpret any expressions in this category. Inversely, since none of these semantics interprets expressions in the domain of type *s*, my new criterion does not count possible worlds or situations as an ontological category. Analogous negative considerations hold for truth-values (or for truth-combinations). I leave a thorough testing and revision of this criterion – and its generalization to a criterion for being a category in the *global* semantic ontology – as a project for future work.

References

Alexeyenko, S. (2015). *The Syntax and Semantics of Manner Modification: Adjectives and adverbs* (Unpublished doctoral dissertation). University of Osnabrück.

Armstrong, D. M. (1980). *Nominalism and realism, Vol. 1: Universals and scientific realism*. Cambridge: Cambridge University Press.

Asher, N. (1993). *Reference to Abstract Objects in Discourse* (Vol. 50). Dordrecht: Kluwer Academic.

Bach, E. (1977). An extension of classical transformational grammar. In *Problems in Linguistic Metatheory: Proceedings of the 1976 conference at Michigan State University*. Michigan.

Bach, E. (1980). In defense of passive. *Linguistics and Philosophy*, *3*(3), 297–342.

Bach, E. (1986a). The algebra of events. *Linguistics and Philosophy*, *9*(1), 5–16.

Bach, E. (1986b). Natural language metaphysics. In R. B. Marcus, G. J. W. Dorn, & P. Weingartner (Eds.), *Logic, Methodology and Philosophy of Science VII* (pp. 573–593). Elsevier Science.

Barwise, J. (1981). Scenes and other situations. *Journal of Philosophy*, *78*(7), 369–397.

Barwise, J. (1989). *The Situation in Logic* (No. 17). Stanford: CSLI Publications.

Barwise, J. (1997). Information and impossibilities. *Notre Dame Journal of Formal Logic*, *38*(4), 488–515.

Barwise, J., & Perry, J. (1983). *Situations and Attitudes*. Cambridge, MA: MIT Press.

Bayer, S. (1996). The coordination of unlike categories. *Language*, *72*(3), 579–616.

Beaver, D. (2001). *Presupposition and Assertion in Dynamic Semantics*. Stanford: CSLI Publications.

Beck, S., Krasikova, S., Fleischer, D., Gergel, R., Hofstetter, S., Savelsberg, C., Vanderelst, J., & Villalta, E. (2009). Crosslinguistic variation in comparison constructions. *Linguistic Variation Yearbook*, *9*, 1–66.

Ben-Avi, G., & Winter, Y. (2007). The semantics of intensionalization. In R. Muskens (Ed.), *Workshop on New Directions in Type-Theoretic Grammars* (pp. 98–112).

Bianchi, V. (2017, 12). *Person agreement, Austinian propositions, and anchoring to the context. ms.* online.

Bochnak, R. (2015). The degree semantics parameter and cross-linguistic variation. *Semantics and Pragmatics*, *8*(6), 1–48.

Bondarenko, T. (2022). *Anatomy of an Attitude* (Unpublished doctoral dissertation). Massachusetts Institute of Technology, Cambridge, MA.

Burge, T. (2005). Frege on sense and linguistic meaning. In *Truth, Thought, Reason: Essays on Frege* (pp. 242–269). Oxford: Oxford University Press.

Cariani, F. (in press). Future displacement and modality. In E. Lepore & U. Stojnic (Eds.), *Oxford Handbook of Philosophy of Language*, 2nd ed. Oxford: Oxford University Press.

Carlson, G. N. (1977). *Reference to Kinds in English* (Unpublished doctoral dissertation). University of Massachusetts, Amherst.

Carlson, G. N. (1998). Thematic roles and the individuation of events. In S. Rothstein (Ed.), *Events and Grammar* (pp. 35–51). Dordrecht: Kluwer.

Carnap, R. (1988). *Meaning and Necessity: A study in semantics and modal logic* (Vol. 30). Chicago: University of Chicago Press.

Cartwright, H. (1975). Amounts and measures of amount. *Noûs*, *9*(2), 143–164.

Champollion, L. (2017). *Parts of a Whole: Distributivity as a bridge between aspect and measurement*. Oxford: Oxford University Press.

Charlow, S. (2014). *On the Semantics of Exceptional Scope* (Unpublished doctoral dissertation). New York University, New York.

Charlow, S., & Bumford, D. (2025). *Effect-driven interpretation: Functors for natural language composition* (J. Ginzburg & D. Lassiter, Eds.). Cambridge: Cambridge University Press.

Chatzikyriakidis, S., Cooper, R., Gregoromichelaki, E., & Sutton, P. R. (2025). *Theories of Types and the Structure of Meaning* (J. Ginzburg & D. Lassiter, Eds.). Cambridge: Cambridge University Press.

Chatzikyriakidis, S., & Luo, Z. (2020). *Formal Semantics in Modern Type Theories* (Vol. 2; C. Retoré, Ed.). Wiley.

Chierchia, G. (1984). *Topics in the Syntax and Semantics of Infinitives and Gerunds* (Unpublished doctoral dissertation). University of Massachusetts, Amherst.

Chierchia, G. (1998). Reference to kinds across languages. *Natural Language Semantics*, *6*, 339–405.

Chierchia, G., & Turner, R. (1988). Semantics and property theory. *Linguistics and Philosophy*, *11*(3), 261–302.

Church, A. (1940). A formulation of the simple theory of types. *Journal of Symbolic Logic*, *5*(2), 56–68.

Church, A. (1951). A formulation of the logic of sense and denotation. In P. Henle (Ed.), *Structure, Method, and Meaning* (pp. 3–24). New York: Liberal Arts Press.

Ciardelli, I., Groenendijk, J., & Roelofsen, F. (2013). Inquisitive semantics: A new notion of meaning. *Language and Linguistics Compass*, *7*(9), 459–476.

Ciardelli, I., Groenendijk, J., & Roelofsen, F. (2018). *Inquisitive Semantics*. Oxford: Oxford University Press.

Ciardelli, I., Roelofsen, F., & Theiler, N. (2017). Composing alternatives. *Linguistics and Philosophy*, *40*(1), 1–36.

Clauberg, J. (2009). *Logica Vetus et Nova (1658)*. Kessinger.

Cooper, R. (2012). Type theory and semantics in flux. In R. Kempson, T. Fernando, & N. Asher (Eds.), *Philosophy of Linguistics* (Vol. 14, pp. 271–323). Amsterdam: Elsevier.

Cooper, R., & Ginzburg, J. (2015). Type theory with records for natural language semantics. In S. Lappin & C. Fox (Eds.), *The Handbook of Contemporary Semantic Theory* (pp. 375–407). Malden, MA: Wiley.

Cresswell, M. J. (1973). *Logics and Languages*. London: Methuen and Company Ltd.

Cresswell, M. J. (1976). The semantics of degree. In B. Partee (Ed.), *Montague Grammar* (pp. 261–292). New York: Academic Press.

Cresswell, M. J. (1990). *Entities and Indices*. Dordrecht: Springer.

Curry, H. B. (1961). Some logical aspects of grammatical structure. In R. Jakobson (Ed.), *Structure of Language and its Mathematical Aspects* (Vol. 12). Providence: American Mathematical Society.

Davidson, D. (1967). Truth and meaning. *Synthese*, *17*(3), 304–323.

Davidson, D. (1977). The method of truth in metaphysics. *Midwest Studies in Philosophy*, *2*(1), 244–254.

Davidson, D. (2001). The logical form of action sentences. In *Essays on Actions and Events: Philosophical essays of Donald Davidson* (pp. 105–121). Oxford: Clarendon.

Dayal, V. (2022). On Chierchia's 'Reference to kinds across languages'. In *A Reader's Guide to Classic Papers in Formal Semantics* (pp. 69–88). Cham: Springer.

de Groote, P., & Kanazawa, M. (2013). A note on intensionalization. *Journal of Logic, Language and Information*, *22*, 173–194.

Degtyarenko, K., de Matos, P., Ennis, M., Hastings, J., Zbinden, M., McNaught, A., Alcántara, R., Darsow, M., Guedj, M., & Ashburner, M. (2008). Chebi: A database and ontology for chemical entities of biological interest. *Nucleic Acids Research*, *36*, D344–350.

Dik, S. C. (1975). The semantic representation of manner adverbials. In A. Kraak (Ed.), *Linguistics in the Netherlands 1972–1973* (pp. 96–121). Assen: Van Gorcum.

Elliott, P. (2017). *Elements of Clausal Embedding* (Unpublished doctoral dissertation). University College London, London.

von Fintel, K., & Heim, I. (2021). *Intensional Semantics: Lecture notes for advanced semantics.* https://github.com/fintelkai/fintel-heim-intensional-notes.

Fox, C., Lappin, S., & Pollard, C. (2002). A higher-order fine-grained logic for intensional semantics. In G. Alberti, K. Balough, & P. Dekker (Eds.), *Proceedings of the Seventh Symposium for Logic and Language* (pp. 37–46). Pecs, Hungary.

Frege, G. (1997). Über Sinn und Bedeutung [On *Sinn* und *Bedeutung*]. In M. Beaney (Ed.), *The Frege Reader* (pp. 151–171). Oxford: Blackwell.

Gajewski, J. R. (2007). Neg-raising and polarity. *Linguistics and Philosophy, 30*(3), 289–328.

Gallin, D. (1975). *Intensional and Higher-Order Modal Logic.* Amsterdam: North-Holland.

Gehrke, B., & Castroviejo, E. (2015). Manner and degree: An introduction. *Natural Language and Linguistic Theory, 33*, 745–790.

Ginzburg, J. (1995). Resolving questions, II. *Linguistics and Philosophy, 18*(5), 567–609.

Ginzburg, J. (2005). Situation semantics: The ontological balance sheet. *Research on Language and Computation, 3*(2), 363–389.

Ginzburg, J. (2008). Situation semantics and the ontology of natural language. In C. Maienborn, K. von Heusinger, & P. Portner (Eds.), *Semantics: Theories* (pp. 267–294). Berlin: Mouton de Gruyter.

Grimm, S., & McNally, L. (2022). Nominalization and natural language ontology. *Annual Review of Linguistics, 8*(1), 257–277.

Grimshaw, J. (1979). Complement selection and the lexicon. *Linguistic Inquiry, 10*(2), 279–326.

Groenendijk, J., & Stokhof, M. (1989). Type-shifting rules and the semantics of interrogatives. In G. Chierchia, B. Partee, & R. Turner (Eds.), *Properties, Types and Meaning* (Vol. II, pp. 21–68). Kluwer Academic.

Groenendijk, J., & Stokhof, M. (1990). Partitioning logical space. Annotated handout.

Groenendijk, J. A. G., & Stokhof, M. J. B. (1984). *Studies on the Ssemantics of Questions and the Pragmatics of Answers* (Unpublished doctoral dissertation). University of Amsterdam.

Güngör, H. (2022). *That* solution to Prior's puzzle. *Philosophical Studies, 179*, 2765–2785.

Gunter, C. (1992). *Semantics of Programming Languages: Structures and Techniques*. Cambridge, MA: MIT Press.

Gutzmann, D. (2019). *Semantik: Eine Einführung*. Berlin: J. B. Metzler.

Hacquard, V. (2006). *Aspects of Modality* (Unpublished doctoral dissertation). Massachusetts Institute of Technology, Cambridge, MA.

Hamblin, C. L. (1976). Questions in Montague English. In B. Partee (Ed.), *Montague Grammar* (pp. 247–259). Elsevier.

Hausser, R., & Zaefferer, D. (1978). Questions and answers in a context-dependent Montague grammar. In F. Guenthner & S. J. Schmidt (Eds.), *Formal Semantics and Pragmatics for Natural Languages* (pp. 339–358). Dordrecht: Springer Netherlands.

Heim, I. (2000). Degree operators and scope. *Semantics and Linguistic Theory (SALT)*, *10*, 40–64.

Heim, I., & Kratzer, A. (1998). *Semantics in Generative grammar*. Oxford: Blackwell.

Hendriks, H. (1993). *Studied Flexibility* (Unpublished doctoral dissertation). University of Amsterdam, Amsterdam.

Hendriks, H. (2020). Type shifting: The Partee triangle. In D. Gutzmann, L. Matthewson, C. Meier, H. Rullmann, & T. E. Zimmermann (Eds.), *The Companion to Semantics*. Oxford: Wiley.

Henkin, L. (1963). A theory of propositional types. *Fundamenta Mathematicae*, 323–344.

Hintikka, J. (1975). Impossible possible worlds vindicated. *Journal of Philosophical Logic*, *4*, 475–484.

Kac, M. B. (1992). A simplified theory of Boolean semantic types. *Journal of Semantics*, *9*(1), 53–67.

Kaplan, D. (1976). How to Russell a Frege-Church. *Journal of Philosophy*, *72*(19), 716–729.

Karttunen, L. (1977). Syntax and semantics of questions. *Linguistics and Philosophy*, *1*(1), 3–44.

Kastner, I. (2015). Factivity mirrors interpretation. *Lingua*, *164*, 156–188.

Keenan, E. L. (2015). Individuals explained away. In A. Bianchi (Ed.), *On Reference* (pp. 384–402). Oxford: Oxford University Press.

Keenan, E. L. (2018). *Eliminating the Universe: Logical properties of natural language*. Singapore: World Scientific.

Keenan, E. L., & Faltz, L. M. (1985). *Boolean Semantics for Natural Language* (Vol. 23). Dordrecht: Springer.

Kim, J.-B. (2008). Grammatical interfaces in English object extraposition. *Linguistic Research*, *25*(3), 117–131.

Klein, E. (1980). A semantics for positive and comparative adjectives. *Linguistics and Philosophy*, *4*(1), 1–45.

Klein, E., & Sag, I. A. (1985). Type-driven translation. *Linguistics and Philosophy*, *8*(2), 163–201.

Kratzer, A. (1989). An investigation of the lumps of thought. *Linguistics and Philosophy*, *12*(5), 607–653.

Kratzer, A. (1991). Modality. In A. von Stechow & D. Wunderlich (Eds.), *Semantics: An international handbook of contemporary research* (pp. 639–650). Berlin: de Gruyter.

Kratzer, A. (1996). Severing the external argument from its verb. In J. Rooryck & L. Zaring (Eds.), *Phrase Structure and the Lexicon* (pp. 109–137). Dordrecht: Springer.

Kratzer, A. (2002). Facts: particulars or information units? *Linguistics and Philosophy*, *5–6*(25), 655–670.

Kratzer, A. (2006). Decomposing attitude verbs. Manuscript. Jerusalem.

Kratzer, A. (2013). Modality for the 21st century. In *19th International Congress of Linguists* (pp. 181–201).

Kratzer, A. (2019). Situations in natural language semantics. In E. N. Zalta (Ed.), *Stanford Encyclopedia of Philosophy: Summer 2019 edition.* Stanford: Stanford University Press.

Krifka, M. (1989). *Nominalreferenz und Zeitkonstitution: Zur Semantik von Massentermen, Pluraltermen und Aspektklassen*. Munich: Wilhelm Fink.

Krifka, M. (1990). Four thousand ships passed through the lock: Object-induced measure functions on events. *Linguistics and Philosophy*, *13*(5), 487–520.

Krifka, M. (1998). The origins of telicity. In S. Rothstein (Ed.), *Events and Grammar* (pp. 197–235). Dordrecht: Kluwer.

Lahiri, U. (2002). *Questions and Answers in Embedded Contexts*. Oxford: Oxford University Press.

Landman, F. (1996). Plurality. In S. Lappin (Ed.), *Handbook of Contemporary Semantics* (pp. 425–457). Oxford: Blackwell.

Landman, M. (2006). *Variables in Natural Language* (Unpublished doctoral dissertation). University of Massachusetts, Amherst.

Lassiter, D. (2012). Quantificational and modal interveners in degree constructions. *Semantics and Linguistic Theory*, *22*, 565–583.

Lewis, D. (1972). General semantics. In D. Davidson & G. Harman (Eds.), *Semantics of Natural Language* (Vol. 40, pp. 169–218). Dordrecht: Springer.

Lewis, D. (1983). New work for a theory of universals. *Australasian Journal of Philosophy*, *61*(4), 343–377.

Lewis, D. (1986). *On the Plurality of Worlds*. Oxford: Blackwell.

Liefke, K. (2014). *A Single-Type Semantics for Natural Language* (Unpublished doctoral dissertation). Tilburg University.

Liefke, K. (2017). Relating intensional semantic theories: Established methods and surprising results. In S. Arai, K. Kojima, K. Mineshima, et al. (Eds.), *New Frontiers in Artificial Intelligence. JSAI-isAI 2017. Lecture Notes in Computer Science* (Vol. 10838). Cham: Springer.

Liefke, K. (2020). Content individuals, truthmaking conditions, and the formal semantics of attitude reports. *Theoretical Linguistics*, *46*(3–4), 267–287.

Liefke, K. (2021). Modelling selectional super-flexibility. *Semantics and Linguistic Theory*, *31*, 324–344.

Liefke, K. (2023a). Meaning-driven selectional restrictions in the difference between *remember* versus *imagine whether*. In R. Loukanova et al. (Eds.), *Logic and Algorithms in Computational Linguistics 2021 (LACompLing2021)* (Vol. 1081, pp. 2–27). Cham: Springer.

Liefke, K. (2023b). Two kinds of English non-manner *how*-clauses. In C. Umbach & L. Jedrzejowski (Eds.), *Non-Interrogative Subordinate wh-Clauses* (pp. 24–62). Oxford: Oxford University Press.

Liefke, K. (2024a). Intensionality and propositionalism. *Annual Review of Linguistics*, *10*, 4.1–4.21.

Liefke, K. (2024b). *Natural Language Ontology and Semantic Theory* (J. Ginzburg & D. Lassiter, Eds.). Cambridge: Cambridge University Press.

Liefke, K., & Werning, M. (2018). Evidence for single-type semantics: An alternative to *e*/*t*-based dual-type semantics. *Journal of Semantics*, *35*(4), 639–685.

Lohndal, T. (2017). Sentential subjects in English and Norwegian. In T. Lohndal (Ed.), *Formal Grammar* (pp. 175–202). New York: Routledge.

Maienborn, C. (2011). Event semantics. In C. Maienborn, K. von Heusinger, & P. Portner (Eds.), *Semantics* (Vol. 33, pp. 802–829). Berlin: de Gruyter.

Martin-Löf, P. (1975). An intuitionistic theory of types. In H. Rose & J. Shepherdson (Eds.), *Logic Colloquium* (pp. 73–118). Amsterdam: North-Holland.

Matthewson, L. (2006). Temporal semantics in a superficially tenseless language. *Linguistics and Philosophy*, *29*(6), 673–713.

Mayr, C. (2019). Triviality and interrogative embedding: Context sensitivity, factivity, and neg-raising. *Natural Language Semantics*, *27*(3), 227–278.

McConnell-Ginet, S. (1973). *Comparative Constructions in English: A syntactic and semantic analysis* (Unpublished doctoral dissertation). University of Rochester.

McNally, L. (1992). *An Interpretation for the English Existential Constructions* (Unpublished doctoral dissertation). University of California, Santa Cruz.

McNally, L., & Boleda, G. (2004). Relational adjectives as properties of kinds. In O. Bonami & P. Cabredo Hofherr (Eds.), *Empirical Issues in Formal Syntax and Semantics* (Vol. 5, pp. 179–196).

Meixner, U. (2011). *Einführung in die Ontologie*. Darmstadt: Wissenschaftliche Buchgesellschaft.

Moltmann, F. (1995). Exception sentences and polyadic quantification. *Linguistics and Philosophy*, *18*, 223–280.

Moltmann, F. (2003). Propositional attitudes without propositions. *Synthese*, *135*(1), 77–118.

Moltmann, F. (2013). *Abstract Objects and the Semantics of Natural Language*. Oxford: Oxford University Press.

Moltmann, F. (2017). Attitude reports, cognitive products, and attitudinal objects: A response to G. Felappi 'On product-based accounts of attitudes'. *Thought: A Journal of Philosophy*, *6*(1), 3–12.

Moltmann, F. (2020). Truthmaker semantics for natural language. *Theoretical Linguistics*, *46*(3–4), 159–200.

Moltmann, F. (2022). Natural language ontology. In E. N. Zalta (Ed.), *The Stanford Encyclopedia of Philosophy* (Winter 2022). Stanford: Metaphysics Research Lab, Stanford University.

Montague, R. (1969). On the nature of certain philosophical entities. *The Monist*, *53*(2), 159–194.

Montague, R. (1970). Universal grammar. *Theoria*, *36*(3), 373–398.

Montague, R. (1973). The proper treatment of quantification in ordinary English. In J. Hintikka et al. (Eds.), *Approaches to Natural Language* (pp. 221–242). Dordrecht: Springer.

Montague, R. (1974). English as a formal language. In R. H. Thomason (Ed.), *Formal Philosophy: Selected papers of Richard Montague* (pp. 188–221). New Haven: Yale University Press.

Moulton, K. (2015). CPs: Copies and compositionality. *Linguistic Inquiry*, *46*(2), 305–342.

Muskens, R. (1995). *Meaning and Partiality*. Stanford: CSLI Publications.

Muskens, R. (2005). Sense and the computation of reference. *Linguistics and Philosophy*, *28*, 473–504.

Muskens, R. (2011). Type-logical semantics. In E. Craig (Ed.), *The Routledge encyclopedia of philosophy online*. London: Routledge. www.rep.routledge.com/articles/thematic/type-logical-semantics/v-1.

Neeleman, A., van de Koot, H., & Doetjes, J. (2004). Degree expressions. *Linguistic Review*, *21*, 1–66.

Ney, A. (2014). *Metaphysics: An introduction*. London: Routledge.

Özyildiz, D., Qing, C., Roelofsen, F., et al. (2022, 04). Cross-linguistic patterns in the selectional restrictions of preferential predicates. Slides from a talk at GLOW 45.

Parsons, T. (1970). An analysis of mass and amount terms. *Foundations of Language*, *6*, 362–388.

Parsons, T. (1990). *Events in the Semantics of English*. Cambridge, MA: MIT Press.

Partee, B. (1983). *Compositionality. Ms* (Tech. Rep.). Nijmegen: Max-Planck-Institute of Psycholinguistics.

Partee, B. (1987). Noun phrase interpretation and type-shifting principles. In J. Groenendijk et al. (Eds.), *Studies in Discourse Representation Theory and the Theory of Generalized Quantifiers* (pp. 115–143). Dordrecht: Springer.

Partee, B. (1992). Syntactic categories and semantic type. In M. Rosner & R. Johnson (Eds.), *Computational Linguistics and Formal Semantics* (pp. 97–126). Cambridge: Cambridge University Press.

Partee, B. (2009). Do we need two basic types? *Snippets*, *20*, 37–41.

Partee, B., & Rooth, M. (1983). Generalized conjunction and type ambiguity. In B. Partee & P. Portner (Eds.), *Formal Semantics: The essential readings* (pp. 334–356). Malden, MA: Blackwell.

Perry, J. (1986). Possible worlds and subject matter: Discussion of Barbara H. Partee's paper 'Possible worlds in model-theoretic semantics: A linguistic perspective'. In A. Sture (Ed.), *Possible Worlds in Humanities, Arts and Sciences: Proceedings of the Nobel Symposium* (Vol. 65, pp. 124–137). Berlin: Walter de Gruyter.

Piñón, C. (1997). Achievements in an event semantics. *Semantics and Linguistic Theory (SALT)*, *7*, 276–293.

Piñón, C. (2007). Aspectual composition with degrees. In L. McNally & C. Kennedy (Eds.), *Adjectives and Adverbs: Syntax, semantics and discourse* (pp. 183–219). Oxford: Oxford University Press.

Piñón, C. (2008). From properties to manners: A historical line of thought about manner adverbs. *Linguistic Society of Belgium*, *3*, 1–14.

Plummer, A., & Pollard, C. (2012). Agnostic possible worlds semantics. In *Logical Aspects of Computational Linguistics, LACL 2012* (Vol. 7351, pp. 201–212). Berlin: Springer.

Pollard, C. (2008). Hyperintensions. *Journal of Logic and Computation*, *18*(2), 257–282.

Pollard, C. (2015). Agnostic hyperintensional semantics. *Synthese*, *192*, 535–562.

Potts, C. (2002). The lexical semantics of parenthical *as* and appositive *which*. *Syntax*, *5*(1), 55–88.

Prior, A. (1963). Symposium: Oratio obliqua. *Proceedings of the Aristotelian Society, Supplementary Volumes*, *37*, 115–146.

Prior, A. (1971). *Objects of Thought*. Oxford: Clarendon.

Quine, W. V. O. (1948). On what there is. *Review of Metaphysics*, *2*(1), 21–38.

Rantala, V. (1982). Quantified modal logic: Non-normal worlds and propositional attitudes. *Studia Logica*, *41*, 41–65.

Rett, J. (2015). *The Semantics of Evaluativity*. Oxford: Oxford University Press.

Rett, J. (2018). A typology of semantic entities. Handout from a talk in the PhLiP seminar. https://rett.humspace.ucla.edu/Rett%202020%20semantic%20entities.pdf.

Rett, J. (2022). A typology of semantic entities. In D. Altshuler (Ed.), *Linguistics meets Philosophy* (pp. 277–301). Cambridge: Cambridge University Press.

Ritchie, K. (2016). Can semantics guide ontology? *Australasian Journal of Philosophy*, *94*(1), 24–41.

Roelofsen, F. (2013). Algebraic foundations for the semantic treatment of inquisitive content. *Synthese*, *190*(1), 79–102.

Rothstein, S. (2012). Reconsidering the construct state in modern Hebrew. *Rivista di Linguistica*, *24*(2), 227–266.

Russell, B. (1996). *The Principles of Mathematics*. New York: W. W. Norton & Company.

Sag, I., Wasow, T., & Bender, E. (1999). *Syntactic Theory: A formal approach.* Stanford: CSLI Publications.

Schäfer, M. (2006). *German Adverbial Adjectives: Syntactic position and semantic interpretation* (Unpublished doctoral dissertation). Universität Leipzig.

Schäfer, M. (2008). Resolving scope in manner modification. In O. Bonami & P. Cabredo Hofherr (Eds.), *Empirical Issues in Syntax and Semantics* (Vol. 7, pp. 351–372). Paris: CSSP.

Schönfinkel, M. (1924). Über die Bausteine der mathematischen Logik. *Mathematische Annalen*, *92*, 305–316.

Schulz, S. (1993). Modal situation theory. In P. Aczel, D. Israel, S. Peters, & Y. Katagiri (Eds.), *Situation Theory and its Applications* (Vol. 3, pp. 163–187). CSLI Publications.

Stone, M. (1997). *An Anaphoric Parallel between Modality and Tense* (Tech. Rep.). Philadelphia: University of Pennsylvania, Department of Computer and Information Science.

Sutton, P. R. (2024). Types and type theories in natural language analysis. *Annual Review of Linguistics*, *10*, 107–126.

Theiler, N., Roelofsen, F., & Aloni, M. (2018). A uniform semantics for declarative and interrogative complements. *Journal of Semantics*, *35*(3), 409–466.

Theiler, N., Roelofsen, F., & Aloni, M. (2019). Picky predicates: Why *believe* doesn't like interrogative complements, and other puzzles. *Natural Language Semantics*, *27*(2), 95–134.

Thomason, R. H. (1980). A model theory for the propositional attitudes. *Linguistics and Philosophy*, *4*(1), 47–70.

Uegaki, W. (2016). Content nouns and the semantics of question-embedding. *Journal of Semantics*, *33*(4), 623–660.

Uegaki, W. (2019). The semantics of question-embedding predicates. *Language and Linguistics Compass*, *13*(1), e12308.

Uegaki, W., & Sudo, Y. (2019). The *hope-wh puzzle. *Natural Language Semantics*, *27*(4), 323–356.

Umbach, C., & Ebert, C. (2009). German demonstrative *so*: Intensifying and hedging effects. *Sprache und Datenverabeitung (International Journal for Language Data Processing)*, *1–2*, 153–168.

Umbach, C., & Gust, H. (2014). Similarity demonstratives. *Lingua*, *149*, 74–93.

Umbach, C., Hinterwimmer, S., & Gust, H. (2022). German *wie*-complements: Manners, methods and events in progress. *Natural Language and Linguistic Theory*, *40*, 307–343.

van Benthem, J. (1991). *Language in Action*. Amsterdam: North-Holland.

Vendler, Z. (1957). Verbs and times. *Philosophical Review*, *66*(2), 143–160.

Vendler, Z. (1967a). Causal relations. *Journal of Philosophy*, *64*(21), 704–713.

Vendler, Z. (1967b). *Linguistics in Philosophy*. Ithaca: Cornell University Press.

von Stechow, A. (1984). Comparing semantic theories of comparison. *Journal of Semantics*, *3*(1), 1–77.

White, A. S. (2021). On believing and hoping whether. *Semantics and Pragmatics*, *14*(6), 1–21.

Winter, Y. (2002). *Flexibility Principles in Boolean Semantics: The interpretation of coordination, plurality, and scope in natural language*. Cambridge, MA: MIT Press.

Winter, Y. (2016). *Elements of Formal Semantics: An introduction to the mathematical theory of meaning in natural language*. Edinburgh: Edinburgh University Press.

Zalta, E. N. (1997). A classically-based theory of impossible worlds. *Notre Dame Journal of Formal Logic*, *38*(4), 640–660.

Zamparelli, R. (1995). *Layers in the Determiner Phrase* (Unpublished doctoral dissertation). University of Rochester.

Zimmermann, T. E. (1985). Remarks on Groenendijk and Stokhof's theory of indirect questions. *Linguistics and Philosophy*, *8*(4), 431–448.

Zimmermann, T. E. (1989). Intensional logic and two-sorted type theory. *Journal of Symbolic Logic*, *54*(1), 65–77.

Zimmermann, T. E. (2017). Intensionale Semantik. In N. Kompa (Ed.), *Handbuch Sprachphilosophie* (pp. 187–197). Stuttgart: Metzler.

Zimmermann, T. E. (2020). *Towards a general theory of type shifting. Invited talk at Semantics and Linguistic Theory 30*. New Haven, CT: Yale University Press.

Zimmermann, T. E. (2022). On Montague's 'The proper treatment of quantification in ordinary English'. In L. McNally & Z. G. Szabo (Eds.), *A Reader's Guide to Classic Papers in Formal Semantics* (pp. 331–366). Cham: Springer.

Zimmermann, T. E. (2023). A compositional version of Kaplan's theorem. Ms. Goethe-Universität Frankfurt.

Zimmermann, T. E., & Sternefeld, W. (2013). *Introduction to Semantics: An essential guide to the composition of meaning*. Berlin: Mouton de Gruyter.

Zuber, R. (1982). Semantic restrictions on certain complementizers. *13th International Congress of Linguists* (pp. 434–436). Tokyo.

Acknowledgments

This Element has benefited from discussions with Justin D'Ambrosio, Jan Köpping, Simon Kreutz, Emil Eva Rosina, Peter R. Sutton, Carla Umbach, Simon Vonlanthen, Markus Werning, Simon Wimmer, and Ede Zimmermann. I thank David Kaplan and Barbara Partee for raising my interest in natural language ontology. Four anonymous reviewers have improved this Element through their immensely helpful comments. I am grateful to our student assistants Yonca Klisch and Jonas Koopmann for their help with proofreading. Finally, I thank the series editors Jonathan Ginzburg and Daniel Lassiter for editing – and providing extremely helpful comments and suggestions – for what would eventually become *two* Elements. Any remaining errors are my own.

For Matti, to help him bring structure into the world

Funding Statement

The author wishes to acknowledge funding from the German Federal Ministry of Education and Research (BMBF) through her WISNA Professorship, and from the German Research Foundation (DFG) through grant no. 397530566, as part of the research unit FOR 2812: Constructing Scenarios of the Past.

Cambridge Elements

Semantics

Jonathan Ginzburg

Université Paris-Cité

Jonathan Ginzburg is Professor of Linguistics at Université Paris-Cité (formerly Paris 7). He has held appointments at the Hebrew University of Jerusalem and King's College, London. He is one of the founders and currently associate editor of the journal *Dialogue and Discourse*. His research interests include semantics, dialogue, and language acquisition. He is the author of *Interrogative Investigations* (CSLI Publications, 2001, with Ivan A. Sag) and *The Interactive Stance: meaning for conversation* (Oxford University Press, 2012).

Daniel Lassiter

University of Edinburgh

Daniel Lassiter is Senior Lecturer in Semantics in Linguistics & English Language at the University of Edinburgh. He works on topics at the intersection of formal semantics/pragmatics, cognitive psychology, and philosophy of language, including modality, conditionals, vagueness, scalar semantics, and Bayesian pragmatics. He is the author of *Graded Modality* (Oxford University Press, 2017) and numerous journal articles.

About the Series

Elements in Semantics emphasizes the field's recent flourishing of interdisciplinary work, connecting linguistics and philosophy with cognitive science, computer science, neuroscience, law, anthropology, sociology, economics, and beyond. The series should be of interest to a broad community of researchers interested in the study of meaning from diverse perspectives.

Cambridge Elements

Semantics

Elements in the Series

Natural Language Ontology and Semantic Theory
Kristina Liefke

Reduction and Unification in Natural Language Ontology
Kristina Liefke

A full series listing is available at: www.cambridge.org/ESEM

For EU product safety concerns, contact us at Calle de José Abascal, 56–1°, 28003 Madrid, Spain or eugpsr@cambridge.org.

www.ingramcontent.com/pod-product-compliance
Ingram Content Group UK Ltd.
Pitfield, Milton Keynes, MK11 3LW, UK
UKHW020904110726
473066UK00023B/788

* 9 7 8 1 0 0 9 5 5 9 6 5 2 *